A Sense of Place

The Society of Women Writers WA

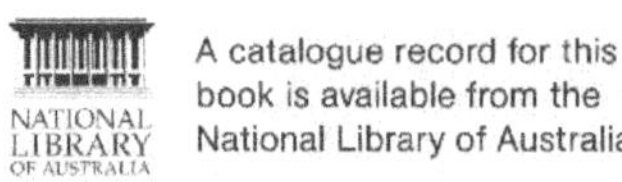

ISBN-13: 978-1-922343-45-1

Linellen Press
265 Boomerang Road
Oldbury, Western Australia
www.linellenpress.com.au

Dedication

This book is dedicated to our beloved Patron,
Mrs Ruth Reid, AM, CIT WA, for her support
and dedication to The Society of Women Writers WA
and its members, all of whom are proud
to call her 'Friend'.

Contents

Acknowledgments

The Society of Women Writers WA Inc would like to acknowledge the following members for their collective efforts in bringing members' writing to publication: the Selection panel – Jan Altmann, Helen Iles, Shirley Rowland, Val McCabe – the anthology Receiving Officer and book designer Helen Iles, and proof reader Maria Bonar. We thank each of you for your role in bringing *A Sense of Place* to fruition.

Foreword

At some stage of our life we make connections, to a person, an object, or a place. Whatever it is, it holds in our memory, remains there for our recall at any given moment. Sometimes that connection invokes feelings of gratitude, elation or remorse, or even inspiration and awe. Whatever occurred in that time, it made an impact, imprinted the images on the author's mind, and held it there so they could relate it at a later date, like now, in this collection of memories of A *Sense of Place.* And 'place' can be a distant location visited, the warmth comfort of a home, or even a sense of belonging to a group.

This anthology holds a wealth of stories, poetry and articles, from established and new authors. It will take you on a journey of discovery to places you might never have been, but will feel you have been by the end of each contribution. You may feel a strong connection just by reading, and feel the author's connection in the details rekindled from memory, and know they truly had felt *A Sense of Place.*

Enjoy!

Helen Iles
Chairperson
The Society of Women Writers WA

The Lion's Mouth

Beautiful, mysterious Venice, famous for gondolas, canals, carnivals, colourful glassware, high art, high fashion and high tides, attracts tourists from all over the world. But in the Spring of 2020 the tourists stayed away, the water taxis stopped running, and the street sellers disappeared. Nature reclaimed the canals which flowed clear and free from pollution, as they had not done for centuries.

The Venice that I experienced though was in the Autumn of 2019. Thousands of tourists waving selfie sticks and clutching shopping bags crowded its bridges, boutiques, churches and coffee shops every day. They seemed to enjoy the bustling activity even though the tide was in, and they splashed around in plastic boots or galoshes. What attracted my attention amidst all this activity, though, were the seagulls sedately swimming in historic St Mark's Square.

Venice is a modern, vibrant city, quieter than most due to the lack of cars and buses, but still very much alive. It is also ancient and full of ghosts. It was the seagulls that prompted me to start looking for these ghosts. The role of birds in the Middle Ages was to guide souls to the afterlife, and I'm sure the gulls of today are still capable of doing the same thing.

The people would have looked different back then, but, just as now, many different languages would have been spoken. Venetians spoke their own dialect of Latin, and their visitors would have spoken Arabic, Yiddish, Persian, and even Chinese. There would have been many visitors because Venice was part of The Silk Road, and this would have brought merchants and traders from China, the Far East, and the Middle East. There were caravans coming and going from Russia and The Netherlands. There would have been Turkish figures in round, white turbans with little red cones on top, colourful robes, and turned up shoes. The Venetians wore long robes too, or perhaps colourful leggings with jackets, velvet hats, and boots. They loved colour, as they do now, especially red, blue and green. I can imagine them weighing out incense and spices, spreading out their colourful carpets, displaying their jewellery and setting out rolls of silk and woollen fabrics on tables beneath large umbrellas. There would have been smells of exotic spices, cinnamon, cloves, and ginger as they cooked their fish on open fires.

There would also have been a few lonely, bedraggled figures wearing simple, brown tunics, little more than rags. Trade brought wealth, culture, and luxury goods, but it also brought wars, intrigue, and a thriving market in slaves. In cultured, Christian Venice, it was legal to buy and sell slaves, so long as they were not Christians. They were brought from Eastern Europe, northern Africa, and central Asia to be auctioned off to the highest bidders. Some were made to line up in the main square, and some were disposed of in private deals in the back streets. Rowing galley ships and carrying large quantities of heavy goods required labour; and ambitious building programmes required men to carry large blocks of stone and marble on their backs. Millions of bricks and tiles were made and laid under the harsh commands and whips of the slave owners and master builders. Between 1414 and 1423 alone, a mere ten years, at least 10,000 slaves were bought and sold in Venice.

Women and girls were included since Venetians were growing wealthy and needed household help. At least this would have given them some food and shelter, but I can't imagine the grief and loneliness of these people (men and women) at being separated from their families and communities for the rest of their lives. I can't imagine, but I know it is written somewhere in the stones and bricks of Medieval Venice. What I can imagine is that the seagulls would have been kept busy guiding lost souls.

Dark and dreadful deeds are embedded in those magical bridges, magnificent statues, and awe-inspiring buildings if you know where to look. Gazing upwards at the pointed arches, the golden mosaics and cupolas of the great Basilica and the Islamic, colonnaded arches of the ducal palace on one side of the Square and then across to the refined pillars of what was once a great library on the other side, I was reminded of T.S. Eliot's observation that 'History has many cunning passages (and) contrived corridors.'

From about the year 1,000, Venice was an enthusiastic participant in the crusades to recapture the Holy Land from the Muslims. Shipbuilders, sailmakers, and rowing crews were needed. Studios and workshops must have been everywhere. The death toll from the crusades was high, but the returns were also high – gold, silver, gemstones, and luxury goods such as stained glass and gilded mirrors, as well as more slaves in the form of prisoners of war.

As a prosperous City State, Venice needed an identity, and so when a couple of merchants returned from their travels to Alexandria in the year 828 with the bones of Saint Mark hidden in a basket of pork so that Muslin assailants would not steal them, Mark was adopted as the city's patron. St Mark's Basilica was built to house his remains, and so Venice gained its patron saint and its identity as the Lion city. The lion (Mark's emblem) is everywhere in Venice.

In 1204, the fourth crusade resulted in abundant booty being brought back, including a set of magnificent bronze horses from St Mark's cathedral in Constantinople. This further established the Republic's position as the most important centre of trade in the west, through which all goods had to pass on their way to

Europe. The city also acquired a great deal of new territory, Byzantine lands, all of which helped to consolidate its hold on the commercial routes that passed through its waters.

Trade and conquest would have been sufficient for prosperity, but brilliant Venice had yet another 'trick up its sleeve,' – double-entry book-keeping. Failing to pay one's artisans, cheating clients out of their rights, and concealing profits from one's masters must have been so rife that there was an obvious need to regulate financial dealings. Help came in 1494 in the form of a Franciscan Friar called Luca Pacioli. Pacioli was a mathematician and a friend of Leonardo da Vinci. He emphasised the importance of balancing income and expenditure. He introduced the use of journals and ledgers and warned that a merchant should not go to sleep at night until his debits equalled his credits.

The day that we took our tour of the magnificent Basilica and Ducal Palace was damp and misty, but at least the tide was out so there was no water covering the brilliantly tiled floors inside. Looking up to the second-floor loggia of the ducal palace from outside in the Square, about half-way along, I could see two red marble pillars standing out from all the white ones alongside them. The guide explained it was from between these two red pillars that the Doge would announce when the next public execution was to take place.

The most notable of these announcements came in 1355. In that year, there was an attempted uprising aimed at installing the current Doge, one Marino Faliero, as a prince. Informants leaked information about this plot to the council of ten, who acted with ruthless efficiency. The plotters were rounded up, tried and summarily executed for treason. They were hanged in a row from the windows of the palace and left there to rot as a warning to anyone else with similar ideas. One of them was the architect who had designed the imposing gothic byzantine palace itself. Doge Faliero was beheaded at the top of the imposing marble staircase that leads into the palace and up to the second storey. His corpse was shown to the citizens before being placed in an unmarked grave, with his severed head between his knees. No wonder I felt uneasy not just at the opulence of the staircase itself but also at the quiet eeriness surrounding it. It was as if the ghost of that unfortunate Doge was still hovering nearby, perhaps still waiting for his special seagull.

Doges acted as governors and magistrates and were elected for life by the city-state's aristocracy. They were assisted by a council of ten aristocrats, who served only a short time in order to prevent plotting or collusion against the Doge. This gave stability, but the ways in which that stability was enforced and maintained were secretive and sometimes savage and brutal.

One of the methods used to maintain order and stability is still to be seen, built into the wall near this staircase. It is simply described as The Lion's Mouth (*Bocca di Leone*). This is a grotesque and sinister image of a demonic face that glares straight out at the viewer with bristling eyebrows and penetrating eyes. The inscription beneath it says: "Secret denunciations against anyone who will conceal favours and services or will collude to hide the true revenue from them." Into this lion's mouth, citizens could 'post' written details of their accusations (usually in the dead of night) of any misdemeanours from petty crime to high treason. By this means, one Venetian could secretly denounce another, if he or she were even suspected of breaking the law. Those making a denunciation were rewarded for their efforts if their information proved correct. Accusations often led to arrest, trial, torture, a time in the infamous prison cells, and finally, a walk across the Bridge of Sighs to public execution by hanging.

The prisons on the ground floor of the Palace consisted of tiny, damp cells, dimly lit by oil lamps, and ventilated only through round holes in thick stone walls through which meagre food rations were passed. The remains of desperate messages can be seen scratched into the walls. There was a shelf for the few possessions, but with no means of bathing and only a wooden bucket for toileting, the smells must have been gut-wrenching.

The Palace is connected to the dungeons by the Bridge of Sighs, so named because its small port-hole windows were to give many prisoners their last glimpse of the outside world as they were taken into prison and then out again to be executed. Some were given fines or short-term sentences, but many more were taken out into the piazza and hanged in public. This took place between two tall columns that support Venice's two patrons, St Theodoro and the winged lion of St Mark. To this day, Venetians do not walk between these two columns. Only the seagulls swim, and watch, and wait. They will not see executions again, but sadly they will be taking care of lost souls because of a terrible virus. But like executions, this too will come to an end, and Venice will become colourful, joyous and vibrant once again.

The Lion's Mouth

Staircase to the Palace

Jan Altmann

On Visiting Graveyards and Other Places Connected to Death

I was four or five when my mother first took me to a graveyard. She may have been searching for a specific grave or had decided to show me the graveyard. I have a vivid memory of a large stone outside the Church gate. It had landed there after being thrown by the giant who lived on Bass Rock, which sits off the Fife coast in the North Sea. You could see his thumbprint.

When we went into the churchyard, in front of the church door, there was a stone table covered in green moss with letters so faded no names could be read. Old and new graves stood down the sides of the church. Beautiful cut grass surrounded them. Some graves were topped by enormous stones with many names, beloved children, or baby, nine months. The older graves had many young children and babies' names on them, a sign of disease and poverty. Fresh graves were festooned in flowers. We went to Crail every year until 1964. I visited the graveyard at least once, if not twice, each time. I never found graveyards creepy.

My mother died in 1964. She was cremated and her ashes placed under a rosebush. I was an adult before I could visit the Garden of Remembrance, in Paisley where she was laid to rest. In 1966, my High School moved beside this cemetery. One gigantic Angel statue stood near the wall. We could see its head. In the dull light of late afternoons, this Angel and its stone cohorts loomed large. Many creepy stories were crafted around these Angels. The boys loved to make the girls scream.

Years later my father took me to Virginia Waters in England to visit the Royal Air Force war memorial. On a hill overlooking a green valley is a large curved wall of sandstone. Silence a presence as my father touched names he hoped not to find. Comrades lost in World War II, no grave their resting place. This sacred space a carved remembrance – for all time – long after those who knew them have joined them in eternal rest.

I find the rows of white markers in the armed services portion of graveyards incredibly moving. White sentinels forever on guard – so many young men lost – Air Force, Navy, Royal and Merchant, Army, Marines. The grave of the Unknown Soldier, representing all who fell and whose bodies were never found or identified, a place for their grieving families to visit and honour their lost loved ones, never found. Wreaths of poppies. Lest We Forget.

And yet I do not find graveyards grim and filled with sorrow. Rather, they are resting places, a reminder that they were once living people. Their gravestones give a glimpse of past lives. Baby died at birth. Child from scarlet fever. Drowned. Mining disaster. Much loved. Beloved. Families reunited after years apart.

These early stones led to the hobby of rubbing headstones. You take a piece of paper, place it over the headstone, and with a graphite pencil or piece of charcoal rubbing over the paper reveals the faded words. This was popular in the Victorian era, a hobby that I would have embraced.

My first graveyards were in Scotland and England. When I was 18 years old, I went on a package holiday to Austria and experienced my first European cemeteries. In small graveyards, the gravestones were more ornate and personalised with the photos of the deceased. Not something I had seen before. In one churchyard, we were told the story of Saint Notburga. Her employer wanted her to stay working in the fields instead of going to church. "Let my sickle decide." When she tossed it in the air, the sickle stayed suspended there. She went to church. On her deathbed, she requested that a cart drawn by two oxen would carry her body to its final resting place. The cart stopped in Eben am Achensee, and that is where she is buried. Saint Notburga from Austria is the patron saint of servants and peasants.

Years passed before I was able to visit graveyards again. In March 2004, I took my husband's ashes back to Scotland to bury him with his mother. She had died a month past her 55th birthday, Jim was 54. The graveyard is small (at least it was then). What stands out is the ages on the stones, so many taken before their time. Only two of the graves were for people over seventy years old. For those of us staring 70 in the face, that is still young. Children's graves with cherubs or toy cars and dolls. Adult graves with little statues of the Virgin and child. Some had cans of beer. Poignant mementos that death can call at any age.

Eastfield Cemetery is down a country lane amid green fields. The sun shone in the chill of March 13, 2004. I had prepared a brief speech, but I think Jim thought it went on too long. Typical Scottish weather, the rain bucketed down. A few days later, we had a sprinkling of snow.

That trip, I revisited Crail cemetery, surprised to find it and the fishing village much smaller than I remembered. An adult's stride is longer than a child's. I still placed my hand on the giant's thumbprint. The engravings etched into the old graves had faded even more over the years.

My daughter and I went to Paris and visited La Pere La Chaise cemetery, a beautiful green space of silence in the middle of the city. Ideal for picnics. A huge carving of the famed lovers Abelard and Eloise topped the first grave that stood out. A metal fence surrounded it. There are many unique graves in Pere La Chaise. Many have tiny houses with a window and door; inside a table and some had altars and some beautiful stained-glass windows. Winding our way between the graves, we found some had no inhabitants but were monuments to those transported to concentration camps. One said, died in Auschwitz. There were memorials to Jews and Resistance fighters.

The grave we looked for was near the top of the hill. There was an attendant beside it. Nearby stands a small hut covered in graffiti. Around the grave were empty beer cans and messages scribbled in chalk, all left by fans. We are at the last resting place of Jim Morrison of The Doors. Many make the pilgrimage to pay their respects. There have been parties. Someone tried to remove his body and other people.

Moving further up the hill, there is a large black slab covering the resting place of Edith Piaf, the little sparrow. I had no more space on my camera and the disposable one as I had gone overboard on the way through the cemetery. Many fans still visit and leave flowers.

There was one more stop. I wished to visit the resting place of the dancer Isadora Duncan. Her tragic ending had impressed me when I saw a film about her life. Isadora was seen by many as the Mother of Modern Dance. She died in 1927, aged 50. Known for wearing long flowing scarves, she was the passenger in a sports car when the scarf flowing out became trapped in one of the rear wheels, pulling her out of the car and dragging her behind it. Her ashes are contained in a box in the Columbarium. The Columbarium looks like rows of mailboxes. Each box holds the ashes; some are for single residents, some are for families.

Among some famous people also buried in Pere La Chaise are Bizet, Chopin, Sarah Bernhardt, Moliere, and Marcel Marceau.

If you visit Paris, then I recommend visiting Pere La Chaise and go for a stroll or even have a picnic on the green lawns. I will certainly go back to Paris revisiting Pere La Chaise plus four other cemeteries of the fourteen within Paris. Many have famous inhabitants.

An old cemetery in Montmartre contains the remains of the

writers Emile Zola and Alexander Dumas and the dancer Nijinsky. The Pantheon in the Ile-de-France has Victor Hugo and the one in Montparnasse has the English playwright Samuel Beckett, the philosopher Jean-Paul Sartre and the composer and singer, Serge Gainsbourg who will be remembered for Je t'aime which made it to number 1 in music charts, outside of France.

In de Pasey resides the impressionist painter Édouard Manet and the composer De Bussey.

However, it is a private cemetery de Picpus that is the biggest draw for me. It is in the grounds of a former convent. Between 14th June to the 27th July 1794, one thousand three hundred and six victims of the guillotine were buried here. One of these is Richard Mique, architect of Versailles who was accused of attempting to save Marie-Antoinette. There is also a reminder that during the French Revolution it was not just the French aristocrats who were sent to Madame La Guillotine. De Picpus is the final resting place of sixteen Carmelite nuns who met with the guillotine on the 17th July 1794. It is reported that the nuns sang hymns and prayed.

In de Picpus there is also an American flag flying above a grave. The French Aristocrat and military officer, the Marquis de Lafayette, who fought for the Americans in the Revolutionary war, was allowed to be buried here because some of his wife's relatives were guillotined during the French Revolution, a pre-requisite for internment in de Picpus. In his coffin was dirt from Bunker Hill, the site of one of the battles of the Revolutionary War. When the Germans invaded Paris during the Second World War, they left the Stars and Stripes flying above Lafayette's grave.

There are a few old Jewish graves outside a small Synagogue in East Perth beside the pavement. Further up the hill is an old church and graveyard with graves from the late 1700s into the 1800s. There are so many Chinese people buried there in one section with no marker.

Outside Northam is a small church and graveyard with many from local families buried there. One moving memorial, a tree, had been planted to honour a son lost in the Great War.

A must visit place is New Orleans, Louisiana in the USA. Due to the water table, the dead are not buried underground, and there are more mausoleums here than anywhere else. Families have been buried here for centuries. Another tradition I would love to witness here is a funeral cortege moving through the streets led by a Jazz band.

Graveyards are not just repositories of the dead, but a glimpse of lives gone by. If you do not wish to leave flowers, maybe a Jewish tradition may appeal. When they visit a grave, they leave a stone to show that someone visited, and the dead have not been forgotten.

There have been four places connected to war that have had an impact on me: two in Scotland and two in Vietnam. Land and buildings can absorb the terror, pain, and sadness that can still be felt years later.

As you drive through the mountains at Glen Coe, there is a heavy sadness that invades the soul. On February 13th, 1692, after spending a week enjoying accommodation and food from the Clan MacDonald and their chieftain Alexander, soldiers of Archibald Campbell, 10th earl of Argyll massacred 34 men, 2 women, and two children. Many of the clan escaped and were able to share the news. The blood and the screams have left a heavy presence that covers the land.

On April 16th 1746, was the last battle of the 45 Rebellion when Jacobites led by Bonnie Prince Charlie, the Young Pretender to the throne, were defeated by William Augustus, Duke of Cumberland. The Jacobites, weakened by cold and hunger, were no match against Cumberland's men who, instead of face to face fighting, stabbed and hacked the ones to the side. After the Battle of Culloden, the Duke of Cumberland was given the nickname of

Butcher Cumberland. Bonnie Prince Charlie eventually escaped to France, where he drank himself to death. When you visit the battlefield today, it is a bleak place where no birds fly or sing.

In both Glen Coe and Culloden, the energy from the blood-soaked ground is dark and heavy.

The Cu Chi tunnels are under the Cu Chi district to the northeast of Saigon, now called Ho Chi Minh City. Thousands of Vietcong hid there during the Vietnam war, popping up unexpectedly to kill the enemy. They laid traps. Some were dugout holes filled with sharpened spikes, or tripwires that set off grenades or landmines.

I expected to feel the energy of death and a gloomy feel to the space. Despite the sound of gunfire from the rifle range in the next field, there is a peaceful air to the setting. I either heard or read somewhere that Buddhist monks had cleansed the area through prayer and bells. Whatever the reason, the atmosphere here gives no clue to the past events.

The exterior of the 'Hanoi Hilton', the prison in the center of Hanoi, gives no clue to what awaits inside. The American prisoners of war nicknamed the prison that. The French had called it Maison Centrale when it was built between 1886 to 1901, and that name still hangs over the main door.

As soon as you pass the entry, the energy begins its effect. The stone of walls and floors are steeped in the blood and cries of the tortured. First, the French, then the Vietnamese, mistreated and tortured the inmates. No part of the prison was exempt from the stain of torture and death. In other prisons, I have visited in the past the execution area where hangings took place, and Death Row, had the dense energy that makes me uncomfortable. In the Vietnam war, the American prisoners-of-war were tortured to try to extract military information.

There is a portable guillotine against a wall which, in one day, killed 13 people. The last prisoner to be guillotined in Vietnam was in the 1960s.

By the end of the tour of the Hanoi Hilton, I felt unwell and on the verge of vomiting. The energy of the Hanoi Hilton is the worst I have experienced. The evils of torture imbued every stone with dark energy. I could not continue with lunch and the afternoon's planned activities. A bath and some quiet time at the hotel set me up, and I was able to attend dinner in a private house – a good end to the day.

There are many places in the world that I would like to visit even though I know they may not be pleasant experiences. Battlegrounds of the American Civil War; Salem, where the witch trials were held; Auschwitz; Port Arthur in Tasmania, to name a few.

Another place I plan to visit is in the south of England, where on some nights, the sound of marching soldiers is heard. Some people have seen shadowy shapes marching along the road. They are only seen from mid knees because they are still marching along the original Roman road. True or not? It would be interesting to find out.

Graveyards, historical buildings, battlefields, share the stories of those who have died and give insights to the culture of those who have gone before. That is why I visit, to touch base with history and the way people lived.

Linda Blackshaw

Rubenesque

Edith entered the Rokeby Road hairdressing salon on impulse. Once inside, the modern chrome and glass decor intimidated her and she would have turned tail and bolted if the receptionist had not greeted her warmly and seated her in front of a mirror.

"Could I have my hair coloured and try a new cut?"

"You certainly can. Our stylist, Miranda, will be with you in a moment."

Two hours later, Edith stepped out of the salon feeling like an entirely new woman. Her eyebrows, lips, and chin had been waxed. Her grey-streaked hair had been released from its tightly wound bun, expertly layered and transformed into a rich chestnut colour with copper highlights. A sparkly clasp secured it in a loose pinned-up style, with soft strands escaping and curling around her cheeks and neck. Her credit card had taken a beating.

What the hell, once I've sold Dad's house, I can stop penny-pinching and live a little.

Edith's staid existence had been transformed in a few short weeks. The old bugger finally carked it and she had taken time off work to clear out years of hoarded junk from his gloomy Subiaco house. She was temporarily living there until the house was ready to be sold.

Thank goodness Trevor the Real Estate Agent suggested I redecorate the place before putting it on the market and introduced me to Sean.

Sean, the handyman, was helping Edith sort out the junk from items that had value, then painting each room as it was cleared. He organised the sale of antique furniture through his trade contacts and advised her to put kitchen items on eBay that she would probably have thrown out, saying "People buy all sorts of retro and vintage stuff these days, particularly in a suburb like Subiaco, where you have these old fashioned character cottages."

She was pleasantly surprised when he proved to be correct. Her father, a Professor of Anthropology in his day, also left quite a collection of artefacts. Sean negotiated a good price for her from a specialist dealer. After a few days working alongside him she had the impression he was flirting with her, but persuaded herself that she was mistaken. Why would this good-looking, younger man be interested in her?

He stayed back late one evening to finish painting the kitchen. Once done, he peeled off his overalls and scrubbed up at the laundry sink. "How about ordering a Thai takeaway from *Six Senses*?" he suggested. "I'm starving and you won't be able to use the kitchen until the paint's dry."

Sean ordered Papaya Salad Soft Shell Crab, Moo Ping and Coconut Prawns, the fragrant aroma filling the house. They drank a bottle or two of Margaret River Sauvignon Blanc, while he charmed her with his amusing stories. Later, he pulled her towards him and melted her heart with his slow, gentle kisses. Before she knew it, she was lying on the sofa minus her knickers, her legs wrapped tightly around him, riding the night away while he murmured erotic words in her ear.

Now, she couldn't get enough of his kisses, his wandering hands and the yeasty smell of him. They paused frequently in their house-clearing and redecorating to fall into bed in the guest room, the scent of frangipani blossom drifting in from the garden. Edith's cheeks flamed as she replayed how skilfully his fingers and mouth teased and caressed all her hidden sweet spots that very morning.

It had been almost thirty years since a man had touched her intimately – and look how that had ended. An unplanned pregnancy; her boyfriend revealing that he was already married, unleashing the full measure of her father's contempt. The reluctant adoption after only a fleeting glimpse of that sweet babe. The annual sorrow and regret on the child's birthday.

Ah, well, she was too old for unplanned pregnancies now. Invigorated by Sean's attentions, she resolved to smarten herself up and make the most of it while it lasted. The renovations would be finished soon and Edith was unsure what the future held.

This morning while twined together in bed, Sean told her "No, you're not fat, Edith, you're Rubenesque, like the woman in your Mum's painting. Men like a handful," he winked, as he fondled her ample derriere.

She had told him about her mother, Frances, finding the old painting on top of a skip outside a condemned house many years ago. How she had rushed home, believing it was a genuine Rubens. Edith's father had mocked her for her naivety. Still, Frances hung the painting high on the dining room wall, where she could gaze at the portrait of the voluptuous half-naked woman while she sat at the polished jarrah table drinking from her china teacup. She enjoyed what small pleasures she had in her short life, succumbing to cancer when Edith was twelve. The fake Rubens, the jarrah table, and her mother's china were the only items Edith planned to keep from the Subiaco house.

She caught sight of herself in a shop window. Her frumpy dress contrasted with her elegant new hairstyle. Instead of travelling to her Fremantle flat as planned, to check her mail and sort out the remaining legal paperwork relating to her father's will, on impulse she decided to treat herself to some new clothes.

Might as well completely max out the credit card!

Feeling reckless, she strolled around Rokeby Road. In *Hidden Lace* she rifled through lingerie in soft silky fabrics, choosing cerise and black lace camisoles, undies and bras. She tried on some plus size outfits in a classy boutique, buying a vibrant turquoise and pink patterned dress with a floaty chiffon overlay that suited her curves. Smart new sandals from *Marie Claire* completed her ensemble. With seduction on her mind, she changed into her new clothes in the shopping centre restroom, dumping her washed out old undies in the bin before heading back to her father's house.

The front door was open to allow fresh air to circulate while Sean painted. Edith hesitated when she saw his legs halfway up the ladder in the dining room. Not wanting to startle him, she waited quietly in the hallway, while Sean talked excitedly on his mobile phone.

"Yeah, mate. I'm sure it's a genuine Rubens. It's very much his style. The signature's faint, but it looks like the real deal and it's got a catalogue ID number on the back. I'll read it to you and you can check it out. Don't take too long though, Trevor. Edith's got the hots for me and *she's* no oil painting. More like the Michelin Man – carrying a few spare tyres," he chuckled. "I have to close my eyes and pretend I'm with my girlfriend so I can do the deed, if you get my drift. In the meantime, I'll keep painting the house and stringing her along. We've made quite a profit on the antique furniture and wow... those artefacts. She doesn't have a clue how much it's all really worth."

Edith's legs trembled and she felt acid rise in her throat as Sean read out the ID number from the back of the painting before ending the call. She heard him whistling as he stretched up to rehang the painting. A storm of rage erupted deep within her and she charged through the dining room door, a 104 kilogram bulldozer knocking the ladder sideways. The painting landed on the floor, while Sean fell awkwardly, his legs twisting through the rungs of the ladder. He whacked the back of his head on the edge of the jarrah dining table with a sound like a dropped pumpkin. His mouth opened and closed like a goldfish out of water and his eyes widened with fear as he tried and failed to breathe. Edith stood above him until his eyes glazed over and his lips turned blue. A stain spread around his crotch and the rank smell of urine permeated the air. When she was sure he was beyond recovery, she picked up the painting and left him there.

She stripped the bed in the guest room and remade it with fresh linen. She vacuumed the floor and wiped all traces of him from the room. Throwing her clothes and toiletries into her overnight bag, she carried everything out to her car, barely glancing at Sean as she departed, leaving the front door open. She would go home and collect her mail as originally planned, do the laundry, hang the Rubens on her lounge room wall, then return to Subiaco tomorrow morning to "find" poor Sean on the floor.

She drove home to her little flat on autopilot, but the sparkling beauty of the sunshine on the Indian Ocean roused her when she approached North Fremantle. She would get over this. She would sell the Subiaco house, look for a better job and treat herself to some more smart new clothes. She would never completely trust another man, but maybe in time she would hook up with someone else. Sean had awakened some deep, dormant wellspring of desire within her. Perhaps Tinder could light her fire? Give her a friend with benefits. No strings attached. It was something to consider...

But there was one certainty; tomorrow she would contact Jigsaw to begin the search for her lost daughter.

Maria Bonar

Haiku

beehive-banded hills
Purnululu campfire smoke
billy on the boil

whale shark hovering
as fishes search the waters
of sea grass meadows

wings of the morning
fly me from the dark of night
to the newborn day

Maria Bonar

I Am

Reflections on
Rottnest Cemetery.

They came, back then, in 1853,
foreheads frowned, heavy tread –
scuffed, scraped my crinkled skin
dug deep into my womb.
Sprinkled Holy Water,
chanted their strange tongue.
Buried him, Luke Ankerman.

They stood awhile. Pronounced me hallowed ground.

Could not they hear the music deep within
that which they were trampling?
My heart, deeply embedded in their grasp, pulsated
a sacredness, mine by right,
bestowed on me by a timeless divinity.

For eons past I've lived and breathed,
writhed, groaned, given birth.
I AM! The Holy One, Mother Earth.

Sun blessed, rain bathed, wind caressed.
In love and harmony, formed this land,
wove a timeless tapestry.
My swollen girth raised up high
mountains, hills, glens and dales.
My breasts oozed water of life,
baptised, consecrated living spirit.

They came again. Thirteen times they came again
to this wee patch they disdainfully claimed
the only place of hallowed ground.
Disregarded my eternal gift: resurrection.

The last time they came,
they gave me you, Patrick William O'Donaghue.

Shackled minds inhibit their capacity
to understand the ongoing mystery beneath their feet,
prevent them from knowing
'twas my dust from which you came,
my tender hand that pushed you forth.
For such a little time, ten short weeks.
Welcome home.

All eventually return to me.
I purge, cleanse and then release
unfettered spirit, breath and hope.
In my heaving bosom, a safe haven, you shall lie
a little while. Wait patiently, you'll soon be free.
You are not alone. Rest assured, I AM, I AM!

Have always been hallowed ground.

Elizabeth Brennan

Sophia

Prostrate upon sun-dappled sand,
count raised veins on my freckled hand.
Surrender own frailty.

Above
the uninterrupted dome, a cloud-free sky, lit by late winter sun …
beckons.
Envelops, warms, raises on high whispered hope.
Dare I succumb to complete abandon?

Sophia, spirit of life and re-generation,
deserts me not to Hades' depths.

Insight bubbles from within, pace with ripples of ebbing tide.
The far-off horizon, no longer a line of demarcation.
Affirms life's boundless gift   hope and salvation.

Naked toes, dug deep in sand,
each grain a page in earth's eternal history,
defy my unwillingness to see my destiny.
A vital component of Sophia's mystery.

I accede.
Anguish, problems I cannot solve   dissipate.

I am released.
Peace and stillness calm the ruffled waters of my mind,
open weary eyes to see anew.

The end must come. Unequivocally.

Awaiting the dawning of another day
I leave this haven, ready to resume my place
allotted me   this moment of time.
I focus on that space where heaven and earth meet.

No longer troubled by its finality.
Mouth a silent prayer.

May I never forget, at least for a while,
Sophia surrounds me with limitless love.
The Great Earth Mother, whose arms above, always there.
Soothe and heal,
despite my moments of doubt and abjection.

With strength renewed
new blood flowing   I rise.
Arms stretched wide, look up.
Indeed, I am not a motherless child.

Elizabeth Brennan

The Oak Tree

A pale sun filters through the stained-glass windows, swathes the pews, imbues them with a shine that belies their age. A dozen mourners, congregated in the back of the church, magnify the isolation of the coffin. A single, small posy of winter daisies cries out in loneliness. The Virgin's face, illuminated in a window above the altar, smiles upon the coffin. The final rubrics complete, the priest pauses. The funeral attendants, conscious of their tight schedule, shift their feet, wait for the priest's direction.

You rise from the back pew, make your way down the aisle to the front of the church.

'Excuse me, Father.'

You hesitate, wonder what on earth you are doing. You half-turn, hesitate again, continue to walk towards the priest.

'I know this may be out of order, but I would like to say a few words.'

The priest stares as you approach him, eyes wide with confusion. You reach the celebrant, address him softly.

'My name is Adam Thornley. I've known the deceased for a long time. Nobody has spoken for her. I left it till now because I … I thought some of the people here … after all, Lydia has lived here for some years … well, I thought one of them might say something. But no one's spoken. Someone must …'.

Your voice trails in your throat.

The priest steals a look towards the pin-striped suited men in the back of the church; nods. You approach the lectern and the priest returns to the presidential chair.

'Please forgive me, ladies and gentlemen. I don't want to take up too much of your time, but I want … I need … to tell you a story.'

A few members of the congregation shift their position, glance at their watches, look askance at each other. A second or two passes in silence. You resume.

'I'm an old man. Yes, an old man, with a long memory. I wish to tell you a story about a girl and a tree.'

You ignore the surprised look on the priest's face.

'It was the most beautiful tree in the garden. Tall and straight, planted in the middle, it commanded a position of power. Its branches stretched out in perfect symmetry, touched the four corners of the garden. Solid, permanent, it exuded a sense of mystery, of wonder.

'Of course, it was out of place: quite illogical to see an English oak tree in the middle of an Australian suburban back-garden. Yet this was precisely one of the reasons that lay behind its beauty. One's eyes immediately riveted to the oak tree, and everything else in the garden, although quite beautiful in their own right, paled in comparison. The oak tree's aura seemed to derive from *its* knowing it should not be there, but it *was* there and there it was going to stay.

'Or so it appeared to Lydia.

'The tree was in her grandmother's garden. She and the tree were one, in nature and spirit. She lived alone with the old woman, who resented the intrusion in her life of this child, deserted by her parents. Lydia lived in a solitary world, one oblivious to her cries of bewilderment and frustration. Just as she often heard her grandmother complain about the oak tree and the space it took up in the garden, the child soon came to know she did not belong, was not loved.

'Whenever possible, she wandered down to the tree, stooped beneath its leaf-laden branches, crawled into the shadow of its bosom. She'd arch her neck, stare upwards, throw her arms across the tree's trunk. Drink deeply of its strength. She'd nuzzle her face in the bark, attempt to stifle her gut-wrenching sobs. Long hours she spent seated at the base, her back against the tree. She'd pick up a fallen leaf, turn it over and over in her hand; grasp an acorn, gently pull it apart, eager to discover, imbibe its mystery of life.

'During the long hot days of summer, she sought relief from the heat under the branches, relished the coolness. When the leaves turned the golden-brown of autumn, she marvelled at the glorious colours, laughed and played among the heap of fallen leaves. She'd scoop handfuls of them, throw them over her head. Sometimes, she buried herself in the leaves, in the same way as another child might bury herself in the sand. Winter did nothing to diminish her fascination. Stripped of its leaves, to Lydia it took on a new beauty as it bared itself to the world, daring all to deny its eventual resurrection. As the winter months rolled on, Lydia tensed with excited anticipation of the transformation to take place.'

You pause, take a step back, retrieve a handkerchief from a pocket. Wipe your face, your cheeks. Screw the handkerchief in your left hand, step back to the lectern, look out over the pews; continue.

'As the years passed, Lydia grew long-limbed, as a sapling. In time, she climbed gingerly onto its lower branches. Bit by bit, year by year, she mounted one more branch, higher and higher, until she reached the top. She'd cling to the upper-most branch, revel in her freedom. The wind swooshed through the leaves, fixed her to the tree. Her grip tightened, she rocked back and forth, back and forth. Never afraid. She knew the tree would not fail her.

'As well as friend, a source of comfort and strength, the tree embodied Mother. As Lydia was rocked and cradled, the tree crooned a lullaby. The lonely girl poured out all her hopes and dreams. Blended with the wine, she shouted from the tree-top:

I'm here, you cannot get rid of me. We are one. The tree and I are one. I'm here to stay. It's my tree. Mine alone. No-one can climb this tree without my permission. My tree! It is me! I'm strong and powerful.

'Healed, strengthened, comforted, loved, Lydia climbed slowly down, satiated for the time being; relished the knowledge she'd return.

'An oak tree takes a hundred years to grow, a hundred years to live and a hundred years to die, her grandmother once told her.

'Those years rolled on. Lydia moved on, away from her beloved tree, from childhood to womanhood.'

Again, you wipe a lonely tear that trickles down your cheek, incline your head towards the coffin.

'Moved on from me, the awe-struck boy who lived next door. The boy who also experienced loneliness, who was too afraid to reach out to this girl he found so awesome, who even if he overcame his fear, did not know what to say. Other than the rare, whispered *Hello* every now and then through the hole in the fence that divided them, the hole through which he spent hours watching her, envying her. The hole in the fence that penetrated his inner being, that gave birth to a love he found hard to voice.

Another pause, another tear.

'A hundred years to grow …! Eventually, I found some courage tucked away deep inside of me, stopped whispering my *Hellos*, found the strength to reach out to her. We became friends, over those hundred years. A hundred years before we felt safe to share our qualms, our fantasies. She shared her love of the oak tree. Another hundred years before she invited me to climb with her. Together we rocked in the wind, laughed together, held tight together. Together … yet still at an unfathomable distance. *It is my tree,* she continually reminded me. *My tree. The tree and I are one. It's roots are deep within my soul. We are one!*

'Those hundred years were not always kind to her. When she finished her schooling, she worked at a few menial jobs for a while. But she needed to leave her grandmother's icy prison, find her own haven. She managed to secure a position as an aid in a residential school for children with special needs. Lydia found her calling. She relished her work, was delighted to help the children find their own giftedness. She called them her Angels. Shy with her peers, with the parents, she opened to the children the depth of her spirit. Instilled in them the mystery of the oak tree. Showered them with love and compassion. They spoke the same language.

'A hundred years to grow, a hundred years to live and a hundred years to die. The years continued to roll.

'Lydia did not marry. It did not worry her that she never fitted in with the *other world,* as she called it. As long as she was with her Angels, that's all she wanted. Life continued to present her with more oak trees to climb, more challenges to overcome. She learned well the lessons of the tree: to weather the seasons of life, to trust in her powers of re-generation. To forge a path amid a hostile environment.'

You heave a weighty sigh.

'I didn't marry either. I could not compete with her Angels. Even though, all those years ago, I climbed the tree with her, unlike Lydia, I didn't find *my* oak tree. That was *her* tree. For most of my life, Lydia was my best friend but I never found the courage – if it was a lack of courage – to cross over into her world. I will regret … do regret that. I never loved anyone else. A hundred years to grow, a hundred years to live … you know how the rest goes. But, I'm not here today to tell you my story. Someday, somewhere, someone … perhaps may speak for me.'

A profound silence has seeped through the congregation. The pin-striped suited men have sat down in a back pew, engrossed in your words, their impatience shunted away. The priest's hands are relaxed in a soft embrace, his eyes closed.

You look over your rapt listeners.

'A few years ago, age and increased frailty more apparent, Lydia left the Home that had given her such joy, a place in which she found fulfillment. With her meagre savings, and with my advice and financial help, she bought the small house in this town.'

You step back from the lectern, drop your head; yet again, wipe your eyes.

'I know that most of you saw Lydia as different. She *was* different. I visited her regularly, here, in this town. I know her seeming independence perhaps threatened you. You probably mistook her aloofness as pride. But she was devoted to your children. And I know they adored her.'

With a piercing stare to the people who begin to squirm, your voice rises.

'I don't know why you haven't brought your children here today. Surely you know how they loved her rambling house, her fairyland garden! Lydia welcomed them into her world, told them stories, wove magic and mystery into their young lives. She shared her own brand of wisdom with them, in words they understood. Urged them to spread their branches, touch the four corners of life's garden. Showed them how to climb, to seek their potential. Encouraged them to permit the wind to rock them, never to be afraid.

'Assured them the oak tree within would never fail.'

Your knees buckle. You grab hold of the lectern, steady yourself; rise to your full height.

'She still offers the same gift, to all of you. An oak tree once sang a lullaby to a lonely, love-bereft child, proved an instrument of healing. This was Lydia's gift. To all who listened. To all who continue to listen. This is her legacy.'

The priest wipes his face, beckons to the funeral directors.

You moved into Lydia's house a few weeks after her passing. At first, the children approached you with an expectation that you would, somehow, incarnate the oak tree within her they loved. Alas, that was not to be. You couldn't do that, and, thankfully, you didn't want to pretend otherwise. It *was* her oak tree, after all. You always knew that.

Something you did know – something you will always remember. You *were* a very special friend. Yes, the oak tree and she were one. But as the hundred years rolled on, you did become aware of how important your friendship was? Were you … are you … mindful of the extent that Lydia relied upon you? A hundred years ago – and maybe another hundred – you were beside her, swaying together, and you both sang in the safety of the tree. You never forgot those songs. Neither did Lydia. She would often hear you hum them quietly when you visited her. A deep smile would spread across her face.

And the adults, the parents of the children who managed to hold on to the lessons passed on to them by Lydia … they have slowly included you in their tight-knit community, offered a quiet friendship, an acknowledgment of Lydia's legacy.

You visit Lydia's final resting place in the small cemetery every day. Your loneliness no longer an issue, you are content to sit there in the silence, embrace the memories that have sustained you, give thanks to an un-known deity for the gift *you* received. You are beholden to the people of the town who have assured you that, when your turn comes, you will be laid to rest with Lydia. You will rest in peace.

There was no fanfare when Lydia came into the world. There was none when she left it. She sleeps quietly in the corner of the cemetery, under a spreading oak tree.

She and the tree are one.

Dear Friend … you and I shall be one.

Elizabeth Brennan

Citizens of the World

I wonder, in this day of instant internet communication when few ever write letters, if young children still write their address, as many did in the past, in this way: House number; Street name; Suburb or town; State; Nation; The World; The Universe.

This seems to echo a dawning awareness of a wider reality, beyond the little world of family and friends. An understanding that this little street leads to a bigger street, to a highway, that links my town or suburb to a city. A city perhaps built beside a river; a river that winds its way down to the sea. A sea that is part of a great ocean stretching far away beyond the horizon, to wash the shores of other lands. Lands where other people live.

People just like us, no matter what the colour of their skins, the food they eat, the clothes they wear or the songs they sing. People who share with us those basic human needs – for food, shelter, and freedom from fear. People every bit as deserving as us, of a right to the pursuit of happiness.

We have been lucky, here in Australia, that, in the words of our national anthem, 'Our land is girt by sea'. And the COVID 19 pandemic explains why that weird line is there. Our 'moat' allowed us to effectively close our borders to the virus, as the nation's founders expected it to keep us safe from invasion. But we can no longer really cut ourselves off from the rest of the world. It is as close as our phones, our tablets, our computers. Television brings it into our living rooms every day.

So, we cannot remain ignorant of what is happening out there, and those capable of feeling empathy for our fellow human beings must grieve for those who live in places where hand-washing and self-isolation are impossible; where lockdown means not just emotional deprivation, but starvation.

How, when geography as a separate subject seems to have disappeared from the primary school curriculum, does the young psyche still seek to centre itself within that broader sense of place? Does the young brain manage to build a mental map, a geographic grid on which to hang the happenings of history and the wars and wonders of our time?

It would be a shame if our younger generations should lose this ability to feel themselves a part of the wider world and build for themselves a truer sense of place – a sense of their place as citizens of the world.

Lynne Cairns

Echuca

We walked down to the river
and followed it up to town.
Saw Emmy Lou get steam up
and slowly pull away
from the wharf.

The old wharf towers high above
the level of the water.
For it remembers other days,
when the Murray River flowed
strong and deep.

A broad road for the paddleboats
that moved the river's trade,
and passengers to ports along
the river's length, back then
in those old days.

The river still will rise in flood
but never get as high
since upstream irrigation
has brought the water level
dangerously low.

Two more new-painted steamers
are lying by the landing,
while others wait for renovation,
and tragic wrecks sink slowly
in the mud.

After coffee at the bakery,
we drove along the river
and found ourselves a campsite
among the ghostly gum trees
by the water.

Lynne Cairns

Sea Song

Our home was built on a high sandhill
I walked barefoot on the sandy tracks
And searched for fairies and butterflies
Among the moss and the winter grass
Under the cypress pines

I remember the scent of the coastal bush
And the constant voice of the wind
Singing and moaning around the eaves
And through the windows, under the floor,
And through the twisted trees

We heard the song that the seabirds sang
And the whispers and groans of the waves
For we lived on the western edge of the land
Where the sea reached out till it reached the sky
And half our world was blue

The song of the sea was my lullaby
And its echoes ring on in my memory
Though I travel far from its sandy shore
The ocean's voice still reaches me
Calling me home

Lynne Cairns

Tree Change

It was just before my tenth birthday that my family left our sandy, wind-blown home at Scarborough Beach and went to live in the Darling Ranges at Mount Helena. A few months earlier, in the August school holidays, we'd travelled up to look at the block. I can't remember much about that first trip, because my memories were to be overlaid many times by subsequent journeys back and forth, but it was all a terribly exciting adventure for us children, who rarely went anywhere except for the obligatory expeditions to visit Grandma in Como. I don't think even my older sister had been on a train before.

The train was pulled by a great, puffing steam locomotive. In fact, there were probably two if it was carrying freight as well as passengers. One locomotive was rarely powerful enough to pull the train up into the foothills, through the tunnel at Belleview and over the Darling Escarpment. The second loco would be unhitched at Chidlow and come back to Perth until it was needed again.

As we chugged up and up, through the rugged, thickly forested hillsides, we had our first glimpses of this new landscape that was to be our home, so different from the gleaming white sandhills, shining sea and scented, grey-green coastal vegetation we were used to.

We arrived at Mount Helena about mid-morning, and the local estate agent drove us out to see the block. Seventeen and a half acres, on the corner of two invisible, unmade roads, off Bunning Road, the bumpy old gravel road that went out to meet

Toodyay Road at Gidgigannup.

To us it seemed a beautiful place that spring, and my mother later said that it looked so lovely and green, not like the beach or the red goldfields country where she and Dad both grew up. They'd also read that the rainfall was forty inches per year. No one told them that all that rain fell in the winter months, the underground water might be unsuitable for drinking, and the lovely greenery was mostly jarrah and marri trees, with an understory of woody native shrubs that would need to be grubbed out before any crops were planted.

But the estate agent had given us some oranges from his trees, so much sweeter and juicier than the sour and withered things our local shop sold, and one of the joys of living in the hills was to be the luscious fruit that loved that soil and climate. Not just oranges and other citrus, but peaches, apricots, plums, figs, and apples

When I think of those first weeks in our new hills home, my strongest memory is of the all-pervading, lovely scent of the gum trees, their tall silhouettes against the sky at dusk, and the fun of camping in two big army tents until Dad built the first bit of our house, so we could move in before winter.

It was only then that I understood the true meaning of 'gravel-rash' and had to learn new ways of walking and running about. For the tiny, orange balls of gravel that covered the ground were never happy to stay in one place and would quickly roll away from under any unwary step, as did the big round 'honkey nuts' of the marri trees. What's more, the resulting impact with the solid, rocky ground was far more painful than my previous tumbles onto the soft white sand of our former home.

Though it was a time of much work and worry for my parents, it was a new and wonderful world for us children. Hemmed in by the tall forest trees, even the span of the days had changed. The sun no longer glimmered on a far horizon at dawn or set in blazing glory over a wide ocean. Now, its rays never reached us until it was high in the sky, and it disappeared behind the forest long before sunset colours touched the sky. That summer, of course, this was a blessing, though the forest also blocked the lovely cool sea breeze that had cooled our seaside home, even before, as the Fremantle Doctor, it whooshed up the Swan River to freshen the air of the city of Perth. Winter was a different matter altogether.

The name Mount Helena dated from some time in the 1920s when, for some reason I fail to understand, it was thought necessary to expunge its old name, Lyon's Mill, from the map. Perhaps the locals objected to the suggestion that they lived in a timber mill town, but timber getters had been active through the district for decades. The fading remnants of their tracks still meandered through the bush, and most of the great and ancient old-growth trees were gone. The tall trees left were those too twisty or stunted to fit the high standards of tall, straight timber needed for building Western Australia's bridges and jetties, and even, sent far away by the sea, to underpin the streets of London.

A few tall old trees had survived though, and during those first few months we had a visit from Mr. Brennan, who lived on the other side of Bunning Road. An old, very skilled timber-feller from the southwest, with only one eye, he came to cut down some of the big trees to provide a cleared building site for our new house. From a safe distance, we watched the process with fascination. Mr. Brennan could control exactly where the tree would fall. Swinging his axe, he made a cut called a scarf in that side of the tree so it would fall clear, then he cut the great tree through, single-handedly, using a crosscut saw. There were no chainsaws back then, and a crosscut was usually used by two men.

The fallen trees were great to climb on, though the Marri bark was very rough and prickly, so not very comfortable to sit on. They were generally known as Redgums, due to the red sap that poured out like blood from any wound. It hardened to a glassy substance. Some of the other plants were new to us, like the strange Xanthorrhoea grass trees, still usually called by the name given them by nervous early white settlers who thought they looked like black warriors armed with long spears. There were Zamia palms with their strange, poisonous red fruit and smooth, thin-shelled nuts, big red and green kangaroo paws (I'd only seen little cats' paws at Scarborough), all sorts of lovely orchids, heavenly blue leschenaultia, purple hovea and many other beautiful wildflowers.

Kangaroos never strayed onto our property, but we often saw brush wallabies nibbling the shoots of our attempts at growing crops. Strangely, I don't remember seeing possums, maybe because all the big trees were cut well back away from the house, and there were so many on the rest of the block they just didn't bother coming around. And perhaps our cats and dogs frightened them and other small creatures away.

The forest rang with the songs and calls of the many birds that made it their home. Often, while tiny wrens and robins hopped or fluttered about, a distinctive call of 'Twenty-eight! Twenty-eight!' would sound as the brighter green of ring-neck cockatoos flashed among the duller shades of gum leaves. Or a cacophony high in the treetops told us that black cockatoos were munching on Marri nuts, with the occasional flash of red tail feathers. One of the strangest forest birds was the tawny frogmouth. We'd heard their booming call, and had been told they were mopokes or boobook owls, but finally discovered they were strange owl-like creatures, with feathers so suitable for camouflage that, by remaining unmoving, they appeared to merge with the boughs they sat on.

As it was summer, snakes were likely to be rustling around among the fallen branches and scrubby bushes, so we soon learned to be very careful where we trod. We were surprised to find that our old friends, the bob-tailed goannas (we called them sleepy lizards) were brownish coloured with orange patches to match the gravel, whereas those at Scarborough had been grey and white.

There was still a week or so of school before the end of the term, so, on Monday morning, my sister and I wandered through the bush to Bunning Road to catch the school bus, which delivered us to the little Mt Helena school. A timber-framed weatherboard building, it had only three rooms and a verandah, so the smallest children were taught in the town hall.

The students were drawn from a wide area, including some smaller towns. Primary-age children were taught in two of the schoolrooms, while the headmaster taught the first three years of secondary school in the one room.

The schoolyard was quite large with a row of tall pine trees across the street frontage and some big, spreading Moreton Bay fig trees between the school and the Headmaster's house next door. We got a new Headmaster the next year, and he was very keen on athletics and hoped to get everyone running, jumping and competing in interschool sports. So everyone had to have a go. Fortunately, if you weren't any good, you could sometimes skip the whole thing. I'm sure my addiction to reading owes a lot to the time spent reading, up in a Moreton Bay fig tree, while the majority of the school huffed and puffed on the oval across the road.

But that was in the future, and for now, it was Christmas time, and no more school till next year. Over the holidays, we obtained a cow, a horse, a small Airedale puppy that we named Gypsy, and a baby pig from our neighbour's farm where he bred tan-coloured Tamworths. Unfortunately, though the piglet was intended as a pet, his mum wasn't very far away, and he kept running home, so we gave up, and he probably ended up as bacon.

My parents' dream of being self-sufficient on a small mixed

farm was never realised, but our tree-change years hold many happy memories.

Lynne Cairns

The Reunions

It was a beautiful sunny day in November; the air was filled with excitement and a great deal of apprehension about how things would pan out. Lester had arranged a reunion of 'Parky Kids' and all residents from the period 1946-1960. The Reunion was advertised in the paper. According to the records registered in Lester's journal about 120 people should attend. It was a good idea, no one knew whether anyone would come, or could come; as memories affect people differently.

As we drove up the hill, up the winding road I felt the butterflies dancing in my stomach. It was a strange feeling knowing how many times I'd come up this same road. Somehow on this day it was different.

"It felt like a lot further when we walked it," my friend Lester said. I agreed with him. He should know, he'd been the second longest resident at the Home. The smell of the gum trees wafted across the road. I breathed in their scent.

As we approached the open area near the front office, I saw the bright colours in the rose garden. Memories again flooded back to me. With tears in my eyes, I pleaded with him to stop.

As he stopped the car I got out and, walking across to the flowers, touched one gently. The years seemed to melt away. I was back there again as a child, feeling the wind start to blow, the unmistakable scent of perfumed roses wafting past my nostrils. I stood there remembering how we would wander around the rose garden admiring the tiny little rosebuds, delicate and fragile, yet long lasting.

"They'll grow up soon," I'd say to Elaine. "All of their petals will open; and they'll spread out and bloom, just like we will one day."

I can see her smiling in my mind, staring at the roses with beautiful brown eyes saying, "I'm grown up now, I'm already big!"

She was turning four soon. I knew I wouldn't be able to call her 'the little one' much longer; not to her face anyway. There in the rose garden I stood with my four-year-old sister, a smile on her face, her bright, brown eyes shining.

"Pick that red one," she would say. "I like red, Nan does too."

On the days when Elaine was crying for our mother, Nan would advise me to take her out to the rose bushes. I stood there remembering how her words were always the same. "June, take her to the rose garden: pick some roses. Make sure you take the scissors, cut off the thorns and wrap them in newspaper. Let her carry them back to me."

For some reason it always calmed her down. Elaine would skip back to the cottage flowers in hand, a huge smile on her face.

"I helped plant those," Lester reminded me, jolting me back to the present.

"I know," I replied. "My uncle Ben told me how he set up the garden beds when he was here; how all the boys kept it going."

"We kept it going all right," Lester said. "They were one of the few things the children could enjoy. There's a rose here for every child who ever found their way here, every time the bushes bloom. On the way back I'm going to pick some of them. I brought my secateurs".

"You can't do that!" I exclaimed.

"Yes, I can," he retorted. "Just remember, I planted these roses; they were for us. Just because everyone saw them as they came to the Home doesn't mean they weren't for us. I've always wanted to pick some

"This is a special place for me," I said quietly. "It has lots of memories."

We walked silently to the open area near the cottages. As we approached, memories came flooding back.

"That's where the swings and a slide used to be," I said. I closed my eyes hearing beautiful music ring through my ears, "Tales from Vienna Woods." I visualise our 20-piece non-tuned percussion band, comprising cymbals, triangles, tambourines, drums and castanets. There stands my sweet little sister in the front row smiling, her beautiful brown eyes shining, her hair tied back with a bright red ribbon, a long black skirt with a red cummerbund, and a white blouse. On her feet are simple black shoes, her face is full of concentration as she bangs the tambourine in time with the music. My brother is standing in the boys' section playing the cymbals, similarly dressed in black long trousers, white plain shirt with a red sash. His hair is slicked back. I'm playing a triangle in the second row, dressed the same, a bow in my hair. Our mother would have been proud of us.

I know from my personal experience that music quells the most troubled spirit. Thank God for May Holt and her musical skills, and her willingness to share them with us. Thank God for the Church of England Sisters who nurtured this gracious lady, teaching her to learn and enjoy music and dance.

The present Director of the Home, Mr. Robertson, welcomed the group, making the facilities of the Home available to us all. To our surprise, he allowed us to access the journals in the main office, which kept a record of our admission and departure date. After taking notes of these details, as well as our own personal medical information, I asked to see my sister, Rosalie's file. Her name had been changed as a young child because of her adoption.

This file was more difficult to trace. When I eventually located her file, it had been marked "SPECIAL FILE". I couldn't find any more information.

As I walked around talking to others, looking at past photos, passing through cottages familiar and unfamiliar, I felt both a sense of belonging and a sense of loss. After all, this had been our only home for eight years, for my brother David and me. Our younger sister had stayed here for four or five years. Sometimes when abandoned, I remember feeling we were part of a large splintered family. The special friends we made, either by choice or necessity, always showed a caring attitude towards each other, especially in times of need. Looking back, I know now that in many ways despite the hardships we endured, working hard before and after school in the bitter cold, we were fed clothed and educated.

I listened to other comments from Parkerville Village School children, grown up now, hearing how they felt about the "The Home Kids". One of my younger sister's friends who attended the reunion told me. "I always felt the kids from the home always came to school clean and smart in the school uniform." Hearing how they felt we all took pride in our appearance, made me feel it was worth the effort. I know the teachers and the Bus Driver felt this way too, remembering their comments: "You always looked so clean and neat, and on time for classes." It seemed like a simple thing to notice. I felt a sense of pride for the children from the Home.

This was something we could do for ourselves, with what little we had. These times were hard for all people. Some of the local families in the Parkerville Village seemed privileged with farms and orchards. I know most of them had to work hard in order to survive and make ends meet. Some of these families were struggling.

To our pleasant surprise, some of the local children from the village, now in their forties and fifties, turned up at the Reunion. One of these ladies came up to me, "Do you remember me? I was Elaine's best friend at school. I'm so disappointed to learn she's not here. I was looking forward to meeting up with your younger sister."

I replied, "I'm sorry, she couldn't come."

I met another visitor who was now a teacher at the local Catholic Primary School. She related to me how the village people felt about the children at the Home. Mostly, she made comments like you were all so well presented, well behaved, clean and well dressed in school uniforms, always such good listeners."

My heart filled again with a sense of pride. Bearing in mind that the previous home background of some of these children, including our small family, was horrendous. I was surprised that most of the past residents looked happy. I thought back to my own experiences realising that if someone guides you, rewarding your individual efforts, this will motivate you strive to achieve.

The rest of the day was taken up with a picnic lunch brought by everyone, a coffee together and a walk around the grounds.

A feeling of calmness enveloped me as I stepped willingly backwards into the past. It was a humbling experience as I stood there looking around at the past residents, some standing quietly looking around for a familiar face, some greeting each other, others already in deep conversation.

'Oh, no', I thought when I saw a familiar face from my high school days. 'I hope he hasn't seen me yet. I don't know what to say to him'. Even though I couldn't remember his name yet, I remembered being responsible for getting him into trouble. It had happened one fateful day when something rude had been written on the blackboard. Initially we thought it was funny. Our teacher certainly didn't, insisting we sacrifice the culprit. Nobody said a word. The teacher stood there glaring at us.

"Alright, own up. Who wrote on the blackboard?"

It was getting very close to lunchtime; we were all hungry as usual.

"If nobody owns up," the teacher said, "you'll all stay in at lunchtime."

Thirty minutes later as the teacher was reading a book, I looked around the room at the desolate faces. My stomach was rumbling, I couldn't stand it any longer. I stood up quietly and said: "It was Clive."

As a consequence, the teacher dismissed the class for lunch, all except Clive who was kept in for the rest of the lunch period. We never knew if he received any other punishment. I knew when Clive gave me that filthy glance he wouldn't forgive me for a long, long time, maybe never.

Clive was always in trouble at school. Unfortunately, I sat in front of him. When he was either making faces at someone or talking in class, the teacher would say, "Duck, June," and a flying missile of chalk or a blackboard duster would whisk past my ear. I was extremely grateful this teacher was a good shot, grateful I had quick reflexes. One day I asked him, "Can I move my desk?"

"No," he replied. "Stay right where you are. I've trained you to duck."

A voice interrupted my reminiscing.

"Hullo, remember me?"

I turned around to face a man with a smiling face, red wavy hair and hazel eyes.

"I remember the face," I answered, taking a second look. This man had faded freckles on his round face, sporting a moustache. He was handsomely dressed in a grey business suit with shiny black shoes.

"You look different, Clive," I remarked as I remembered his name.

"You don't," he retorted. "I would recognise you anywhere."

"I thought for a moment you had forgotten me," he quizzed.

"How could I forget you, Clive? Your face is etched in my memory, you were always in trouble at school." His smile faded. I could have bitten off my tongue when I followed up with: "You were such a rat-bag."

"Well, Miss Good Goody Two-Shoes, it was better than being the teacher's pet. You were never brave enough to do anything wrong. I still remember the day you dobbed me in to Mr. McMahon for writing on the blackboard."

"If you'd been brave enough to own up in the first place, you wouldn't have been in so much trouble," I justified. "How do you think we felt being punished because of you?"

Suddenly Clive laughed and reached over to give me a big hug, saying, "Anyway I forgive you. That happened a long time ago. Besides, teacher's pet or not, I know you worked very hard at school. You deserved to succeed."

By this time, we felt better, moving on to more pleasant memories. I learned from Clive he was a Company Director. 'It goes to show that anyone can succeed if they put their mind to it', I thought.

At the end of the day after looking at photos, cottages, graves, sharing memories with each other, everyone exchanged phone numbers and addresses, vowing to keep in touch. As the past residents wrote their information in the journal, talk was already going around about holding the next get-together. Those who attended enjoyed the day immensely, thanking Lester for arranging the Reunion to share our past experiences. Talking to each other that day we realised the sense of family and belonging that was so desired by all of us, valued above all else.

It was strange leaving the Home at the end of the day, knowing that we were free to leave at any time without seeking permission from anyone. We had become our own people; we controlled our own destiny.

The second reunion was arranged by the 'Friends of Parkerville', as a request was made by the older generation to become involved. It was held a few years later, a Church of England Bishop held a service in the Chapel for the past residents, including the previous generation. As I stood in this Chapel, memories came flooding back of the countless hours I had spent in this peaceful place throughout my stay at the Home. Sometimes this church felt like a sanctuary, especially when things didn't seem right. A visit to this place would help to quell my anxiety.

As I sat there with mixed emotions, listening to the Bishop paying homage to the dedication of the Anglican Sisters for the hardships they endured, I felt a sense of peace within. Significant people from the 'Friends of Parkerville' were chosen for readings at the service, the hymns chosen carefully for the service. I was surprised how we knew the words to all of them. I could feel the strength of the bonds that these people had, the special bond forged in their childhood experiences. Immediately after the service the previous generation mingled with our group.

"I know who you are," I heard a voice behind me. "You're Caroline's daughter. You look just like her."

I was very surprised at this, after such a long, long time. I had only distant memories now, memories coloured by me over time.

"She was such a lovely person," she continued.

"I know," I confirmed.

As I listened to the conversations around me, I could hear that these past residents had lots of stories to share about their life's experiences, some filled with joy, others sad.

Like the first Reunion we had an open invitation to enter any of the cottages, two of which were set up with photos and information about the home. It was possible to buy copies of the photos, as well as a couple of books that had been produced about the home. Vera, one of the original children, was just completing a biography of Sister Kate, who originally founded the home. Most people bought these smaller books. There was much discussion about the faces in the photos. Friendships were renewed. I remember meeting one of May Holt's friends. She approached me saying, "I knew your mother as a child, you look a lot like her." I couldn't help asking questions about my mother.

Everyone told me how soft and gentle she was, working hard to keep us together as a family. All of them mentioned her long black hair, dark eyes, that she was tall, slender, and very pretty. This confirmed all my memories I had of her; I still yearned to find out more. "Has anyone any photos of Caroline?" I asked.

"Sorry, May Holt was the only one with the photos." I found out later May had shared all of her photos with her friends a long time ago. They were lost to me now.

We knew of gravesites just outside the Home, graves of children who had died at the home in the early days. Originally there were numbers on the graves, and written records of the children buried there. We were not able to look at the journals this time, to ascertain which children were buried at the gravesite. No one seemed to know then what happened to the records of the children buried there.

A bus took us to the gravesites, way out in the bush. A man in his fifties was designated to guide us. He explained there had been a bush fire scorching some of the white crosses on the graves. One of the members of the group, who had previously worked at the farm, kept staring at Stan, the tour guide. As we listened intently to his voice he asked, "Don't I know you?"

"Probably," the man replied with a shrug, "I've been here forever, all my life. As a teenager I worked on the farm. I decided to come back. Since then, I have been the Farm Manager, providing food and vegetables for the Home."

Immediately, half a dozen boys remembered growing up with him. "We remember you, Stan, we worked on the farm too." Eventually, Stan announced it was time to return to the Home. Quietness came over us on the way back from the graves. I remember feeling very sad for these lost children. I feel sure that the Sisters did all they could to help them recover. This place was so isolated, infectious diseases were rife in the early days.

The visitors spent the rest of the day mingling, sharing tales of their experiences, relating incidents from their past that were important. Many at this Reunion confided in others, disclosing how their circumstances led them to being admitted to this home, how long they had spent there, and how they had fared.

The older generation were small in number, having very interesting tales of hardship to relate, some being very grateful for being rescued from difficult home situations. Listening to some of the conversations, I felt there were not too many past residents showing resentment about being abandoned here as a child, most had seemed to come to terms with their predicament. Possibly, those that felt resentment chose not to attend the Reunion. There will always be stories from some past residents feeling they were mistreated as individuals, some of these incidents staying with them forever.

Most of the visitors stayed for the whole day, leaving when the cool evening air set in, thanking the Director of the Home for organising this second reunion.

We drove away from a place that in a lot of ways was more than The Home, it was our home.

June Cornock

Rosalie's husband, Lionel, and me at the Parkerville reunion.

Night Shift

Torn fishnets
Legs crossed at the ankle
High red stilettos
More than a little worn
She takes a long drag on the menthol cigarette
Savours the hit of nicotine

Low black sports cars and SUVs prowl the night
Occupants hunting for prey
Some keeping watch on their girls
Window down
Arm resting on car door
He slows
Hesitates
Her cue

She pushes off the wall
Engages her walk
Hip sway over exaggerated
Leaning in
Rests her ample bosom on open car window
She's distracted by the rat scampering past her feet
In a drain embellished with the filth and grime of life
Cigarette butts, condoms, food wrappers and piss

The john looks like all the others
Mr Average
Mr Family Man
He speaks
White noise to her
A flash of cash

She's on her back
Dreaming of first morning light
When she can go to her bed
Above the Chinese restaurant
Above her grimy world
Above the men
The low lives
The drugs
The feel of degradation
Till night comes again

Lucy Cotton

The Manor

Permission to step ashore, Sir? Words I long to hear again, on distant sunny days.

The June storm rages from the north. Winds capable of knocking a man clean to the ground whip across the top of the limestone outcrop of my island.

'I hope the little penguins survive the night.'

'Don't concern yourself, Jacob,' I reassure my trusty companion. 'They'll be in their cosy rock ledges watching over a precious egg.'

I check the fuel in the Kerosene lamps that hang about our humble dwelling, which I like to refer to as The Manor. A hessian cloth serves as a door. My cot in the corner tempts me for a nap, but I need to get the rabbit I've skinned and gutted in the pot if we are to eat tonight.

I'm always the cook. No doubt Jacob would be capable, but the task fell to me. Or, if I were honest, I felt I did the better job. Jacob knew me well enough that there was no malice.

Once the stew is underway, I mix flour, sugar, lard and water by hand in a coconut shell that serves me well as a bowl. A souvenir from my travels around the globe. Damper to dunk in the stew will help fill our bellies.

My favourite cable knit jumper, a gift from my wife, and the kerosene cooker keep me warm and grateful to be inside. Jacob sits in the corner, rubbing gloved hands together, more out of habit than cold.

I open a bottle of cheap red wine that I obtained on the

mainland earlier in the week, sloshing it into tin ramekins. Approaching nights like tonight warrant a drop of comfort. It would aid our slumber.

'Shouldn't you be checking on the afternoon crew, Sir?' asks Jacob.

'As if I'd neglect my duties,' I rebuff. The birds are everything to me. They are like family. Residents long before I found this wondrous place. Pelicans, Silver Gulls and Terns to name a few. Sea Lions and Bottlenose Dolphins visit us on a regular basis, but for me it's the birds that lay claim to my home. And I am a generous man, happy to share it with them.

Glimpses of white cloud peek through blustery grey skies. Sunset will come early today. The days grow shorter. Without consulting my pocket watch, I'm aware it's nigh on four in the afternoon. Pelicans approach as they do each day on their return home. Flying low above the chop of the waves in a V formation, wings spanned wide. They are a majestic bird.

'All present and accounted for,' I inform Jacob.

'Thank you, Sir. Good to know.'

Jacob is a man who enjoys things orderly and accounted for. This type of chap suits me as a companion.

For a young man, he is an unobtrusive fellow. He showed up one day and stayed. I found him wandering on the back beach of the island. In fact, if you ask me where he hails from, I could not tell you. We have a mutual respect for each other's privacy. What has passed in our lives before matters not. Even in the peak of summer when guests pour onto the island, Jacob stays in the background. I suspect he doesn't want to show himself through either a shy disposition or a shady past.

Enjoying the last of the natural light, I run my weather-worn fingers over the frayed slip cover of my book. Robinson Crusoe is a tale I never grow weary of. If I had to be honest, I have considered myself as adventurous as Mr Crusoe. And I did sport as fine a beard and moustache as he, if I say so myself.

The stew proves delicious and fills our hungry bellies. The rabbits, although destructive to the habitat, are a blessing to the cooking pot this time of year. The catching of fish and squid in winter months is not as productive as the warmer days.

I reach for the bottle of wine to fill my cup, but alas it is empty. Possibly for the best. Jacob and I move closer to the kerosene cooker, enjoying the last of the warmth.

The sound of waves smashing into the sandbar on the east side of the island makes our cave more inviting. Both of us aware of the wailing sounds no doubt coming from Singing Rock, a small rock outcrop between us and Seal Island.

'Tell me again, Sir, what happened to her,' pleads Jacob, who never seems to tire of the tale.

'Well, Jacob, local legend has it that long ago a young Noongar woman and her lover came to the island. He was from an opposing tribe. Her elders chased them to the next rocky outcrop where they were both killed. Ever since, locals have called it Singing Rock. She's calling her lover on the wind.' We both sit in reflection for a while till Jacob shifts the mood.

'I remember the day you became King of Penguin Island, Sir,' he says with a wide smile.

'Do you, my boy? You disappeared during all the festivities.'

'Oh, but, Sir, I missed nothing from my observation post.'

'You mean that big old fossilised Tuart trunk near North Rock?'

I could see from the look on Jacob's face, he was reliving the grand day in his head. So I indulge him, as I have done on many occasions.

'What a fine day it was.' I rub a forefinger along the bristle of my moustache. 'The local folk, crossing Mersey Point in their wooden boats, dressed in their Sunday best. A couple of young chaps made their way on foot across the sandbar, water lapping high at their legs, their tweed jackets held above their heads. We couldn't have had better weather.'

'The ladies looked lovely, Sir,' Jacob comments then blushes as if he's spoken out of turn.

'Indeed, they did, Jacob. I greeted each one of them on bended knee as they dismounted onto the shore, kissing their hand in greeting. And their men folk, paying their respects, requesting permission to come ashore.'

'You looked grand, Sir, in your red cape and crown of ivy seated on your makeshift throne. The crowds cheering. The music and dancing that followed.'

'What a wondrous day, Jacob.' I turn from the warmth of our cooker and rub my eyes. 'Damn fumes. Makes the eyes watery.' In reality, the memory still moves me. It had been a glorious theatrical event. Although conducted in good humour, it had meant that the locals accepted me, this wild man of many travels, hailing from Nova Scotia.

My whole life I've had the wanderlust. The world and its people I've found to be favourable towards me. In particular, this Great Southern Land. It welcomed me as I came in poor health, having contracted a fever whilst making my way through China. My time spent working in the state's northwest had been one of mateship and hard drinking. As I made my way further south, the year 1914, I stumbled across the little coastal township of Rockingham.

Would I ever go home? I often wondered. But where was home? I'd left a wife and children behind in New Zealand. Did they miss me? Had they mapped out new lives for themselves?

Jacob and I attend to our ablutions and made ready for our beds.

'Goodnight, Jacob. Sleep well.'

'Good night, Sir. See you at sunrise.'

In 1914, Paul Seaforth McKenzie unofficially took up residence in the caves on Penguin Island, located 45 minutes south of Perth, Western Australia. He was said to be charming in nature and in 1918 granted an annual lease from the Western Australia Government to establish a holiday resort in the island's many caves. He left the island in 1926, returning to his wife and children in New Zealand. The crowning him King of Penguin Island is an actual event. The character of Jacob is fictitious.

Seaforth McKenzie

1918 - 1926

Lucy Cotton

Seasons in Le Riols

Short sharp gunshots ring out across the dense oak forests that cloak the hills surrounding the small French village of Le Riols. As I open the bedroom windows and swing back the blue wooden shutters I can hear the flapping of pigeons rising from the church steeple and the chasse dogs yapping at the wild deer that has been shot by the hunters. It's a bright shining Sunday morning in autumn and the ancient wisteria shading the terrace is sparkling with droplets of moisture and shedding its leaves when the wind blows. A skein of mist hangs between the river in the valley and the tree tops, indicating a fine day.

Every day the church bells chime at 7.30 in the morning, 12 noon and 7.00 pm, disturbing the pigeons clustered on the steeple. The swallows gather on the wires for their winter migration south, chirping as they swoop around the house.

These are some of the sounds that highlight the passing of time and the changing of the seasons in Le Riols, a tiny hamlet located on the banks of the Aveyron, the border between two Departments. The village lies to the east of the ancient Duchy of Aquitaine and is north of the region famous for the Cathar religion in medieval times.

The locals speak French with an Occitanie accent and the village is identified as 'un village occitanie.'

In autumn, the sounds of hunting, wood chopping and chain sawing are the predominant noises, signalling preparation for the cold winter months – the need for meat and heat. The largest logs are piled by the side of the road, others are stacked neatly in backyards or on the edge of fields. Armand piles his carefully inside his orchard fence. The smell of wood fires drifts around the village in the early morning as stoves are lit to warm the ancient stone houses. Antoine's old tractor rattles through the village towing a homemade trailer filled with logs.

There is the distant hum of tractor engines as they plough in the remains of summer crops like maize or are planting winter wheat. Monsieur Compere, who is at least ninety, uses a rickety noisy tractor that is a World War Two survivor to transport him between fields, puffing out dirty smoke from chimney stack and exhaust. He has a stall at the Varen weekly market selling autumn produce like pumpkins, cabbages and knotted carrots with real clots of earth on them. He grunts 'bonjour' when spoken to but little else as he weighs the vegetables using a hanging metal hook and saucer, the ancient article clanking as he picks it up off the table.

In autumn, two newly fledged barn owls perch side by side at dusk on the telephone wire outside the house. Through the open window at night I can hear them communicating with each other, the sound like heavy breathing. They disappear after a few weeks as they hunt for prey in the thick oak woods.

On the last weekend of October, the local village called Laguepie holds the Marche de la Chataigne, the chestnut fair. Accordion music is heard in the cafes where locals gather to exchange gossip or talk about illness or the impediments of old age. The predominant sounds are voices, young and old, gruff and gentle, friendly and chatty.

The buzzing sound of conversation surrounds the stalls as requests are made and news exchanged of families and friends. The stalls are laden with vegetable plants for winter, intricate wire work and handwoven straw baskets, seasonal fruit and vegetables including a grand selection of pumpkins. Chestnuts and walnuts are piled loose in baskets and rattle as they are served by the kilo.

Traffic is blocked off so children chase each other around the streets, their excited voices ringing in the clear air and echoing from the old stone buildings. In the middle of the village the rush and ripple of two rivers converging, flush with early autumn rains, mingle with the splash of water tumbling over the weir up river. Birds cry and call as they land on water and grass or fly up to chimney pots and church steeples.

Church bells announce the first day of winter and November which is named Toussaint or All Saints Day. Locals gather in the village, parking their small cars in the centre and by the cemetery. Their friendly voices greeting each other fill the village and small children cycle by with a family dog following behind. The children always stop to greet people as it is French custom to acknowledge people at gatherings, in markets and shops. The villagers walk in groups to the tiny cemetery and gather around their stone family tombs, many embellished with photos or icons of Mary and the saints. The flowers placed on the tombs are always brilliantly coloured pots of chrysanthemums bought at local markets.

After their devotions are made the people slowly move into the Salle de Fete – the village hall – where long tables are laid with food and wine provided by them. There is no need for background music as the murmur of voices is enough. People wander in and out, smoking or chatting or visiting the village toilet opposite. By late afternoon the cars depart and the village becomes tranquil again.

The church bells ring again on November 11, Remembrance Day and the locals arrive, the hum of cars parking and the comforting sound of people greeting each other fills the village place. A brief service commemorating the dead of World War One is held by the Mayor at the recently erected war memorial and fresh flowers are laid at the base. The villagers gather afterwards in the Salle de Fete for lunch, their voices dimming and increasing as they move in and out of the hall.

The village church uses different peals of bells for special occasions like Toussaint, weddings and funerals. In mid-November the bells ring continuously for a funeral before the church service, during it and for a set period afterwards. The locals gather outside the church porch, sign a book of condolences and gather in groups to talk quietly. People acknowledge each other with a nod but no words, hugs or kisses.

Their attitudes reflect solemn respect for the old lady who had lived in the village all her life and died last week.

The village resumes its tranquillity as winter approaches. A few locals take walks and tractors rumble through the middle. Hugo and his friend cycle furiously, followed by their loyal dog, calling to each other and us as we wave. The truck bringing central heating oil stops in front of the house, engine running as the driver unwinds his hose to pump the oil direct into the tank in the cellar. The engine noises of other trucks delivering fuel and the baker calling to his customers briefly disturb the pigeons on the church steeple and the voices echo off the stone walls. On Wednesdays, the clank of garden tools disturbs the peace as the gardener starts his work, often interrupted by villagers exchanging news and views.

A group of older couples arrive in the village centre on Thursday afternoons for the 'the dansant' in the Salle de Fete. Tables are pushed aside and they dance to lively traditional French music played on an accordion, the sounds of their enjoyment flowing out of the open doors.

Nearer to Christmas the locals gather one morning to hoist up the Christmas tree in the village place amidst personal greetings, laughter and shouted instructions to ensure that it is located correctly and the lights are strung around. When it is finished, they disappear into the Salle de Fete for pizza and wine as usual. A small boy walks over to the tree in the dusk and jumps up and down with happiness.

Next day in early evening Antoine, dressed as Papa Noel, drives his tractor towing a trailer decorated with Christmas lights around the village. On the trailer are kids and parents and recorded Christmas carols.

After, Christmas snow falls silently on rooftop, road and field and there are few tractors and cars. The only sounds are the croak of crows and cooing of pigeons, the occasional tuneful song of robin or blackbird. The village hibernates and people stay indoors, only venturing out to the regular Saturday market.

Spring is a welcome relief as the days become warmer and garden birds like the colourful chaffinch, the robin and blackbirds sing, chirp and warble from dawn to dusk. The swallows return and swoop in twittering clouds around eaves and rooftops. House martins squeak as they rebuild nests in the eaves. Cuckoos welcome spring from the wooded hills with their distinctive call and pheasants cark as they run across fallow fields. Woodpeckers drill intermittently in the oak woods.

The village is woken at dawn by the farm cockerels crowing and the lone donkey braying for his food. The chasse dogs, now securely chained in backyards, join in the noise with their yapping. The farmers are busy and tractors crisscross the village all day. The villagers attend to their vegetable patches and the first groups of cyclists and hikers liven up the village with their chatter as they pass through.

Local tradesmen, supervised by the Mayor, bring tools, ladders and materials to spend the weekend mending the public toilet roof. There is much lively discussion before they start. Their wives help by washing the old terracotta canal tiles as they are removed and handed down the ladders. They all stop for a simple lunch in the Salle de Fete including wine. The village gardener works all day on Wednesdays in the central place, the cemetery and roadside verges, putting plants in stone pots, mowing, weeding and talking to locals.

The weather is kind, gentle rain pattering on the new leaves of the trees and the wisteria in the backyard. The spring wind has lost the harsh cold of winter and blows down the lanes and around corners, causing the new growth to ripple in the fields and the chestnut trees to sway their leaves. Local markets are busy as villagers gather to exchange news, their cars parked in neat rows on gravel spaces. Some wander down to the river to sit on metal benches and watch the swallows swoop over the water and ducks swimming frantically against the spring flow. The flapping of heron wings is heard as they gather in the heronry and call to each other whilst building their nests.

The village cafes are full of locals sitting out on the pavements enjoying the spring sunshine. There is no recorded music to impede conversation. There are handwritten notices on village noticeboards advising dates of specialised markets for garden and vegetable plants, roses and exotics.

In spring the first vide grenier markets are advertised in nearby towns and villages where people set up makeshift stalls and sell household goods, antiques and collector items. The stalls are placed outside houses or in allocated areas like fields, village centres and streets. They are well patronised by locals, visitors and holiday home owners seeking cheap furniture for vacation cottages. Local producers of wine and oil, honey, homemade crafts, wrought iron and garden furniture are regular attendees so there is much exchange of news and views with friends and relations.

Great black iron cauldrons of paella, stews and casseroles are selling portions for a minimal cost and the vineyards offer wine tasting and special deals. A local accordion player provides music for a group of school children. It is a celebration of village community life and the start of warmer weather as the vide grenier markets continue to the end of September. Local cafes spread their tables and chairs onto pavement and square and children chase around as traffic is blocked from the roads.

On Midsummer's Day, 21st of June, the whole of France celebrates with a musical fete providing a varying quality of music from live bands to taped pop and disco music. By daybreak in Le Riols, Antoine attaches his old trailer to his tractor and loads it with the wooden tables and benches stored in a garage opposite the Salle de Fete, rattling past my house. Locals are chattering and laughing as they gather together, bringing in food and wine for the midday repas which they take to a shaded parking area down the road where there is a permanent shed housing a bar for occasions like this. Wine and beer are sold in paper cups and is very cheap. Regis plays his accordion whilst people eat and afterwards a few couples dance on the square concrete area. The village is quiet in the afternoon as villagers rest in preparation for the night-time festivities which can go on till dawn.

In July and August summer thunderstorms are violent in the region of the Midi-Pyrenees. The sky darkens with bruised purple clouds and lightning flashes in forks and streaks across the sky and glows above the horizon. Thunder roars around the wooded hills as the storm follows the rivers and rain lashes the countryside. The storms are dangerous and have caused the whole electricity system in a building to crash and blown out a stone wall. Fortunately, the church opposite my house has a lightning conductor. Often the storms are at night so we light plenty of candles and firmly shut the solid wooden shutters over the windows to protect the old glass, switch off the TV, Wi-Fi and all electrical items. These storms can continue for hours as they circle the hills and rivers.

When the hot wind, the sirocco, comes from the south it brings dust from the Sahara which coats vehicles and window ledges, sprinkles leaves on bushes and trees. The ground in fields is hard and large irrigation equipment stretches across them, sucking water from the rivers. Luckily, we have picked the sweet wild blackberries and plums flourishing on hedges in fields and by the roadside. The local wives are making jam in copper cauldrons perched over gas rings in rickety old wooden sheds.

On the first Sunday in August, Le Riols always holds its Vide Grenier market. It is considered to be one of the largest in the area with 120 stalls, some being trestle tables, some with wares laid out in vans or on blankets on the ground. The whole village is closed to traffic once the stall holders have set up. They arrive by 7.00 am and there is an air of festivity in the village amidst door banging, dogs barking and people laughing. It is an important community event patronised by locals and visitors. In 2015 the vide grenier was wiped out by 4.00 pm as a hailstorm swept across the valley of the Aveyron, carrying hailstones bigger than golf balls. They caused immense damage, smashing car windscreens and bonnets, wing mirrors and house windows.

The local newspaper printed pictures of motorists stranded in country lanes surrounded by mounds of hailstones.

A week later, the nearby village of Laguepie holds its vide grenier along the river banks. It includes a demonstration by an old threshing machine and a display of antique tractors. The streets are lined with local producers and La Troubadour Café expands across the village place. People walk around munching on pizzas, homemade confectionery, pastries and baguettes. The weather is hot as it is the second Sunday in August but the two rivers converging add coolness to the shaded areas on the bank. It is a time to meet friends and villagers, holiday house owners visiting for the summer months with children and dogs in tow. The only sounds are peoples' voices and children running and yelling as traffic is blocked from the village centre.

A wedding is held in the village and the peace is disturbed by the hooting of cars, and a large black truck decorated with ribbons and balloons rounds the bend and parks by the church, blocking the road. It is surrounded by well-dressed wedding guests and smiling locals.

The Mayor conducts the service from the steps of the Mairie. He is smartly dressed and some of the locals have changed their track suits for tidy trousers and shirts but still wear worn old leather boots with mud and straw clinging to them. We are asked to join the guests by the Mayor's partner and everyone claps at the end. The happy bride and groom walk down to the church and photographs are taken. The late summer sun is shining benignly through the leaves of the plain trees and birds warble their song. It is an idyllic scene. The wedding party disappear into the Salle de Fete for their feasting. Children run in and out, kicking a ball or chasing a dog, the parents looking on with smiles.

All too soon autumn comes again and the village plain trees shed their crinkly brown leaves which pile up on our house steps, crunching as we walk down. The swallows are amassing and twittering on the telephone wires preparing for their winter migration to Africa. Combine harvesters are completing the harvesting of maize and tractors are ploughing the fields. Driving through the narrow lanes is tricky as huge harvesters can suddenly appear round a bend in the road filling it from building to building. Soon the sounds of chain sawing in the woods, gunshots and chasse dogs disturb the village tranquillity.

The gardener is working hard sweeping up the leaves and humming to himself. Ian takes his guitar and I bring a chair and we join Gilles in the village place singing 'Autumn Leaves.' Michel, the deputy Mayor, laughs and joins us. Antoine wanders around from his house to enjoy the music.

The falling leaves drift by my window.
The autumn leaves of red and gold.

Alison Croft

Unhomed

Since you left, our home is not the same. I have not changed anything, but it feels empty without your presence. Your clothes are still hanging in the wardrobe, but you are not there to wear them. On the walls are your paintings which remind me of your creativity. Your chess books line the shelves, but you are not around to study them. Even when I switch on the TV I cannot escape the hollow sensation of life without you. I have no-one to comment on the programs, to discuss the merits of the movie. There is a vast gaping chasm I cannot fill. At night I lie in bed alone. Sometimes when I awake after having a bad dream, I reach out for you to comfort me, but there is no warm flesh to feel. There is no-one to reassure me.

At first, I thought you might be making a fuss when you said your voice had changed, and it was difficult to articulate the words. The E.N.T specialist gave you extensive tests but could find nothing untoward. 'Sometimes as you age the muscles are slack,' he said.

You practise Thai Chi daily. 'I can't raise my right arm,' you say.

'Maybe you strained it when you carried the case on our holiday in Broome,' I say. 'Lucky you are left-handed.'

When you have an x-ray they do find a tear in the tendon. 'It takes time to heal,' I say. When we walk you must rest on the bench because you feel so tired. The heart specialist can find nothing wrong.

You are referred to a geriatric specialist who sends you to a neurologist. 'I have the results,' the specialist says.

'But I don't know whether I should tell you now, just before the festive season.'

'You might as well,' my husband says, 'as now you've mentioned it we shall only think the worst.'

'You don't have Alzheimers, or Parkinsons. You have Motor Neurone Disease.'

'Like Steven Hawkins,' I say.

'But he has an unusual form of it,' the specialist tells us.

'How long have I got?'

'Two years at the most,' he tells you.

We drive down to the river, both of us in shock. 'I'm 83. I've had a good life,' you say.

'We must make the most of every day,' I say.

The sun is shining, reflections of light on the water, the trees impervious to our plight. We go home.

Despite the limitations we try to enjoy each day. The children visit us more often which is some compensation. Using your left hand, you manage to dress yourself, shower, you play chess, and we watch movies on TV. But your spine becomes bent like an old man, and we are loaned a walker by the MND society who are very supportive. You don't complain; your attitude is stoical. I do my best to look after you as I see your faculties diminish.

'You can have a PEG, a feeding tube, inserted if you want it. Some people don't bother,' the specialist says.

'I will try,' you say. The will to live is still strong in you. They teach me at the hospital how to prepare the feeds. I've never been dexterous but I learn. They give me encouragement. They say 'You are doing well.'

We still carry on and my close friends come from over East to visit you. We all eat while you have the feeding tube. 'I have no appetite,' you say.

One morning it's much worse – you can't move. You tell me,

'I don't think I'll last too long.'

The nurse sends for an ambulance. At the hospital you seem at first to stabilise. The children, and grandchildren visit. We can't understand your speech any more. You can just about write on a white-board. But now you have difficulty breathing.

I say to the nurse, 'I can't find my mobile, I'm lost without it.'

You write on the white-board. 'You're lost without your phone … I hope you won't be lost without me.'

The nurse asks, 'Do you want a morphine drip?'

You nod your head. I sit beside you and say, 'I love you.'

I hold your hand until you fall into a deep sleep. After a few hours you are still sleeping so I go home. In the morning the nurse phones and tells me your breathing has changed. As I go towards your room she intercepts. 'Sorry, he's gone.'

You are lying on the bed, a shell of your former self. My son takes me home. The funeral is arranged and it doesn't seem real.

Now that everyone is busy with their lives, a change has come over me. We were married for over 60 years and we courted for three years before that. I know for your sake I must carry on, that's what you would have wanted. Now I am comforted to have your things around me. If I don't know what to do, I only have to think about the good advice you would have given me. I'm not alone any more. You are part of my consciousness.

Pat Curtis

Butterfly

Lips painted deepest plum
rusty hair knotted chaos
she circled Freo market
flaunting a splash of shawl.

Butterfly hands caressed a swirl
of gypsy skirt, finger tipped
a speck of stilton, grazed
fresh baked sourdough.

She lingered at a bookstall
read aloud discarded poetry
musty pages seasoned
with age spots.

Her voice was earthy
textured with rich vowels
releasing fettered words
that rose and fell

to languish beside her carrier bag
full of yesterday's untasted crumbs.

Geraldine Day

Word Sleuth

I have waited for words draped
against the Sydney Opera House
nestled in a secret garden
at The Rocks savouring the summer
wine slither of linguine and, yes, I have felt
their sharp blue-iced edges on Franz Joseph.

I inhaled them amongst damp pungent colours
of Vermont, on subway clatter in New York
an image found in Times Square, lost
in wild remnants of a hurricane.

I glimpsed a sestina in the slow
motion of an ancient gorge
the weathered glass of a crocodile's eye
the dawn shadows of Purnululu.

I searched, stumbled, smelt words
in the coffee crush of a Montmartre market
cobbled alleys and olive groves
tasted them in a handful of sunsets.

Maybe I'll ride a thermal to Santorini
follow signposts on a footloose journey
into the arms of a dark eyed lover.
Then, surely, a poem will find me
shape its own language of mosaic
verbs across a breathless sky.

Geraldine Day

Along the Track

Along the track kangaroo paws circle smoke bush
an eagle soars over untamed land
where a ribbon of gravel unfurls
through paddocks of yellow canola
and purple lupin.

Beneath sailboat clouds
adrift in a sea of blue
weeping willows create an oasis
along the river bed
for pink and grey galahs.

Willy wagtail sits on the old bull's back
in a herd of cows
ears flicking flies
oblivious to the shrill screech of corellas
jostling on power lines.

Everlastings pink, yellow and mauve
turn daisy faces to the sun
and wattle dust creates
yellow streams
in corrugated grooves.

Weathered signposts salute scattered farms
beyond the scrub
where sheep graze and flock for shade
under distant gum trees
along the track.

June Earle

Highland Intruder

The first rule for wildlife photography is patience. Lessons learnt come to my mind as I scramble over bumpy tussocks of grass and rocks. I wonder how animals keep their balance – right now I could do with an extra pair of legs.

I am surrounded by the highlands of Scotland where the weather constantly changes and repaints the landscape. My aim is two stags making their way up the mountainside. Below, the motorhome is diminishing in size. Trevor will now be curled up with his book and a hot mug of tea. Another rule of photography: don't wait for the right weather. As the cold bites and the wind threatens to topple me, my mantra is, *I am not a twit; I am not a twit.* Trevor has given up when I say stop – he does and waits in comfort as I dash about with my trusty camera.

Below, the loch is slashed with a shaft of silver as wind ruffles the surface. Collapsed dark stones, a battle lost, squat at the water's edge. Time and tide gnaw the ruin. The trek is wet and mushy. I'm almost on my hands and knees now as the climb steepens. The stags have stopped – bless them; I am running out of breath.

They observe me as I watch them; I take up position on a narrow skirt of rocks, choosing a granite ice block to sit on. A trickle of water slops a percussion of clops as it finds its way to the loch. The larger of the two stags paws the ground; the other shakes his antlers. Puffs of steam spurt from black noses. My backside is numb, but a shift in posture could disturb them. It's a standoff in the highland corral and I need to get the first shot.

I feel their uncertainty. I do not belong in this landscape. Patience comes to mind again – it is a waiting game.

Ears prick, liquid brown eyes stare at the intruder, a quiver runs along the red hides. Then heads drop to nibble grass – I am accepted. My notes appear like the course of an erratic spider – fingerless gloves are good but not in this weather. I remove the camera from beneath my coat and deflate the Mae West bosom. In the silence comes space for thought, the sense of freedom is fabulous.

Behind closed eyes, I imprint this visual feast on my memory bank. Misty vapour circles peaks; there is a musty smell of dank peat mixed with a pungent stench of soggy grass and lichen. Above, aisles of starchy white slide down crevices. In this intimate stillness I appreciate the great creator.

My stags are on the move. They pause, stand for a moment and gaze back at me. I capture the image worth waiting for.

I thank them for allowing me to share their highland home as a curtain of sleet blurs their retreat. My legs threaten to strike: you don't have to be dead to be stiff.

I hear Trevor's comeback whistle. The thought of a whiskey – without the ice – spurs me on.

June Earle

Skomer Island, Wales

Skomer Island in Wales is a resort for birds. It guarantees every nest and burrow a scenic view, and the abundant fish supply ensures a cuisine to suit every beak.

Part of the Pembrokeshire coastline, the 292 hectare island, is managed by the Dyfed Wildlife Trust. In late spring and summer, sheets of Bluebells, Thrift and Red campion carpet the island; thrive in soil made nitrogen rich by seabird droppings.

Walkers stride quiet tracks, hoping for a glimpse of the little reddish Skomer Vole, an appealing animal not much bigger than a mouse, that scuttles through the undergrowth in search of seeds and insects.

We find here many species of birds, providing the photographer and birdwatcher a grand vista or intimate detail. In the breeding season there is a concentrated frenzy of feeding and rearing of fluffy chicks. We observe the flight prowess of birds from several cliff vantage points. Below, Grey seals, their round heads sticking out from the water; watch with big-eyed curiosity as birds stumble and fall in slow throbbing flight and call to each other.

A black-legged Kittiwake stands on one leg, bobs and twists while cleaning its plumage. Overhead a Skylark serenades us. We stand in awe as this plain bird with a variance of trills and whistles leaves us speechless.

Cliffs of Skomer Island are thick with guillemots, razorbills and puffins. The sky is full of their mutterings and calls. Kittiwakes rise against the sky like a puff of grey smoke; change in an instant to a cloud of snowy steam as they dart around in unison. Flying in and out, puffins with orange feet tucked into soft white undersides, wheel, turn and poise like children let loose in the playground. As the green lungs of the sea breathe, the duck-like guillemot's float, and then lift to fly on rapid whirring wings. Once on land, with their long paddle feet stuck out in front, they stand in chatty groups like small penguins at a party. Above the murmur of the waves, another Skylark sings a never-ending melody.

On the grassy slopes of the island, puffins provide entertainment. A puffin, his beak full of sand eels, pauses a moment as though reflecting on the glory of his catch. With big sad eyes, over a bizarre coloured-stripe bill, he views the world. On land puffins totter like miniature Charlie Chaplains on a rolling deck. Polite, they are always giving way. They seem to say, "Pardon me, were you here first? So sorry, after you."

Mated pairs greet each other with affectionate pecks. A delight to watch, they chisel dirt with their beaks and shovel out burrows with webbed feet; communicate through groans, growls and grunts. Excellent swimmers, they see above and below water; they fly on wings that seem to have difficulty supporting their squat bodies; careering towards the sea until the rapid beating of wings takes effect.

A cry goes up. Someone has spotted a Peregrine falcon. People sprout like mushrooms; a line of tripods edge the path. The amateur and professional share the spectacle, binoculars ready. The Peregrine flies with perfect control. A swift dive with closed wings, the deadly accuracy of the falcon triumphs as he captures a puffin and flies off.

Visitors stand and gape at the aerial antics of the Chough. Recognisable, with red beaks and legs, a handsome bird with glossy blue-black plumage. Their *Chee-ow* calls fill the air. Head and body vertical, they shoot skywards with the up-draught, somersault and plummet down with folded wings; level out seconds before hitting the sea, leaving spectators breathless.

Inside the ruins of the farmhouse built on the island in the early 1800s, short-eared owls have made a home. Their charming appearance belies their efficiency as killers. The soft, downy, big-headed birds hide cruel talons beneath feathered trousers. The rebuilt cowshed has information on walking trails and wildlife. Maps on ancient monuments built in the iron age when Skomer Island was part of the mainland around 35,000 years ago are interesting.

Great black-backed gulls bully puffins into dropping their catch. Their grim shadows send the little clowns into noisy hysteria. It is a tremendous sight as the launch leaves the greenstone bulk of the island. Heady with the pure air and the experience, Skomer Island will remain one of my favourite places to revisit and recommend.

The best time to visit is from April to mid-August. Take food and drink as they limit facilities to one place. It's a wild place with spectacular scenery for a picnic lunch. Wear a hat as bird droppings are common. Book with the Dale Sailing Company, it is only a fifteen-minute launch trip to reach the island, weather permitting. Accommodation is available on the mainland in Dale, and Marlowes.

June Earle

Highland Time

A curtain of mist veils our view, draws closer. We drop speed. Narrow and winding, a single-track road demands attention. Another set of headlights penetrates the gloaming, reaches the passing place before us and waits. Hands are lifted in acknowledgement, a courtesy encountered in this terrain.

We are only halfway to our destination on a road that cuts through a hazy view of blackened boulders in boggy moorland. We think back to the ferry crossing two minutes' sailing from the mainland to this wild peninsula, the light still with us shining on loch and bracken. Now eeriness as the long twilight begins.

As we come round a bend, a magnificent stag, crown of antlers held high, bounds through the undulating land on our right and is then obscured by one of the enormous rocks on this countryside. As the road straightens out, he comes into view once more and leaps across our path, too close to the windscreen, scaring us but romancing our journey.

This then is Ardnamurchan Peninsula in the Scottish Highlands, close to Fort William. It is the most westerly land mass of the British mainland, twenty-three miles further west than Land's End. We are here because an artist friend in central Scotland has gifted us a week in a former schoolhouse now belonging to her family.

Hours later, we come to a potholed lane signalling we are reaching Achosnich – to speak its name is to tickle the throat with Gaelic. The cottage lies in its own tiny valley, huddles in the curve of the nearest hill. Our arrival is greeted by Blackface sheep. Light is now failing. We unload what we need and insert the key in the lock of the sturdy grey stone house, leaving the darkness behind to climb a carpet of muted turquoise wool woven by Kirsty, our generous friend.

Morning brings blue skies, scudding clouds and, through a gap in the hills, a sparkle of sea. We find we are surrounded by a landscape going back to glaciers and volcanoes whispering us into the past and the heart of things. No other humans around, only sheep which move reluctantly to allow us to make a pathway to our car.

Three miles to the west is Ardnamurchan Point with its lighthouse and a jagged coastline bitten by Atlantic fury. At the coast the sand is fine in texture, pale gold in colour. The beach is empty of people, full of nature: bird calls, waves lapping on this day, roaring on others, taste of salt in the air, smell of seaweed, shiver of wind. The peninsula feels like an island in its isolation. The real islands are out there, part of the Inner Hebrides: Rum, Eigg, Muck and Coll, all easily seen on clear days of that week. They recline like slumbering seals.

Sky here is giant in nature, untamed and of whims. Nimbus cloud freaks to cumulus then whisks to cirrus. Blue appears disappears; wind gusts, restores. Nature resounds with crashing, beating of waves, booming of thunder. And yet, there are lulls of silence and peace in this place of wind and water, earth and light.

Our week in October is charmed. When we go walking, rain falls after we return, always clears up quickly to be followed by bright sun. We bake bread and have soup simmering for homecoming. From the window we watch the light change as the sun appears, disappears and we sit by the fire reading or talking about this experience in a wondrous landscape.

One day we visit the island of Mull, a thirty-five minute sail south from Kilchoan, a short journey from our cottage. The main town on Mull is Tobermory, situated round the harbour. As we disembark, we can see the shopfronts famous for their palette of various colours and much photographed for Scottish calendars. The pinks, yellows, greens and blues are a welcome contrast to days of grey in sky and sea. But today blue plays with cumulus, patterning sky and sea shimmers. We wander round the town and visit the distillery where there is a warm welcome and an offer of a 'wee dram' of peaty Tobermory whisky.

Another day we drive eastwards into the peninsula to Salen, a Gaelic name which gentles the tongue. Then there is Ardtoe, a fusing of Gaelic and Norse. We see few people in this landscape; have the golden beach at Ardtoe to ourselves and enjoy walking on the unspoiled sand, savouring the pure, fresh air. Weather, isolation and the power of nature dominate.

The small things in life become important, rhythms change, time stands back. Awareness heightens: cry of peewit, chill of chattering burn, taste of freshly caught trout, smell of peat in the hearth. Senses take over, induce calm.

At Kilchoan, our nearest hamlet, the farm shop has a notice: Shop closes at 5 p.m. We arrive fifteen minutes late, ring the bell and, before long, the proprietor and his dog make an appearance. 'Are we too late?' we ask. His reply encapsulates our week on Ardnamurchan. 'No, no, not at all. 5 p.m. is only a guide. We're on Highland Time'.

Blackface: a breed of sheep in Scotland and elsewhere in the U.K.
peewit: lapwing
burn: a small stream or brook

Margaret Ferrell

Sanctuary

Full moon, and a sky spread with diamonds,
banish sleep, so I walk that ancient way
past whitewashed cottages
then through wrought iron gates
to come to that quiet place beside
a fast-flowing river.

Larches stand tall; even in moonlight
their leaves flame reds and golds.
Breeze silks my skin
gentles movement in trees.

Close by are relics of
once tall columns –
on the wind a faint chanting.

Once a place of carnage, anguish,
today peace wraps round ruins –
sound of rushing water,
crunch of Autumn leaves underfoot.

I return along the street heavy
with history, long restored after tumult.

A blackbird – opening the dawn
chorus – fills his throat with music.

My eyes open to morning's light.

Margaret Ferrell

Published in WA Poets' Creatrix Journal 38 September 2017

Winter

north

A cloud of white breath
bruises ice on the window.
Frost stiffens grass
yet snowdrops shelter mosses.
Slip of sunlight,
a melt of frozen puddles.
Trees bare, waiting;
grey space weaves between branches.
Temperature rises
brings snowflakes, slow and large –
drifting a white silence.

south

A storm growls in
from the Indian Ocean.
Wind wails, rain whips
windows, but next day a high
tears clouds to show blue,
lucent sky. Surfers tower
waves, pavements sprout
café tables, owners serve
lattes, tagliatelle and smiles
Air crackles with chatter
as sun warms.

Margaret Ferrell

Published in WA Poets' Creatrix Journal 35   December 2016

Beverley Springs
now known as
Charnley River

It took us two hours to negotiate the 43k. road to Beverley Springs. The first half was easy driving, and we wondered at the dire warnings we'd received. Twenty kilometres in we met the grader returning to his camp which we passed at the turnoff from the Gibb River Road. Two kilometres on, the road abruptly deteriorated into rocks and ruts and running water – mutilated, sometimes obliterated, by five months of rain.

Barry later confessed he'd been tempted several times, to turn back, especially on the last 15ks. But with thick mud and dense bush on both sides, it wasn't an option anyway. I have no recollection of being scared; only of discomfort and some anxiety as we pitched, swayed and battled the track through floodways still loaded with water from the recent cyclone. Three things allayed fear – there are no savage animals in Australia; help was only 20ks. away, and Barry had his GPS.

When we passed a helicopter parked on an airfield, and the track changed to harder surface, we relaxed and breathed again.

The tourist information brochure enthused about scenery which required a whole day to take in, and recommended phoning ahead about accommodation, which indicated to me that it was a popular spot. So I did as instructed and asked for a campsite for one night and what was described as a "rondaval ensuite" for the next. I did wonder at the time why the woman I spoke to sounded dubious, but concluded she was trying to fit us in.

We did a circuit of the seemingly deserted homestead, trying to decide which was the front entrance amongst a ramshackle cluster of connected huts. We chose a set of steps that looked more front-doorish than the rest, and found a screened verandah with windows and doors leading to the inside where we could hear a couple of men talking. A woman answered our knock.

Maybe they thought we were lunatics either of the raving mad kind or of the violently psychotic type. She didn't open the door, and we were a little disconcerted at being told to drive that way, skirt the windmill, take a left at the fork, and the camp ground was straight ahead. Barry was given instructions on how to prime the water pump for showers and toilets.

We did as directed, and found ourselves in a cleared area about the size of a football ground, vegetated only by prickles. A mob of curious kangaroos watched from a safe distance. Not another camper in sight.

With daylight vanishing, we found a scrubby tree on the edge of the field, not too far from a dilapidated building, and once Barry had worked out how to achieve running water, I had a hasty cold shower while he set up camp.

During this activity, a ute appeared and drove slowly around the perimeter, scaring off the 'roos. It stopped a little away from us. A man emerged and Barry went over to see him. He'd brought us some firewood, and wanted to check we were okay. Was he merely curious, or did he wonder if we had gone into hiding, ready to attack the homestead when everybody was asleep? He must have deemed us harmless, because we were invited to come up to the homestead next morning, and could move into the rondavel immediately.

Their curiosity and/or suspicions were probably not surprising. In our ignorance we had no idea that the huge properties up north (Beverley Springs is 750,000 acres) are vacated for four months of the year during the wet season. We learned from the station owner, that he travelled by helicopter, and supplies are brought in by plane, with a look that implied only tourists are silly enough to brave the road. They had returned to the property only two weeks before, and, as far as they knew, their access road was still not negotiable. The appearance of a small semi-off-road vehicle carrying two middle-aged city types may well have seemed unusual.

We headed back to our camp before darkness closed in, downed a couple of well-earned beers, ate spaghetti and meat balls, and were in bed by 7.30. I must confess to feeling a little nervous that night, hundreds of kilometres from civilisation and at the mercy of the elements and wildlife. But knowing that the local fauna was unlikely to either eat or trample us helped, and the very fact that we were so far from civilisation also eased my nerves.

On the other hand, it was a strange, almost exhilarating feeling to be way out there in a part of the planet so remote that few people would ever have been there. The rest of the world probably had no idea it existed.

The night was still and there was no moon. No fire, no lights, no reflections, only the sky heavy with a billion stars that seemed to be watching over us. I felt isolated, alone, but neither lonely nor unsafe. If there was another reality, we gave no thought to it. Exhausted by a tough day's driving we were asleep by 8pm. At least, I was.

The birdlife of Greater Oz woke us early next morning, with squawks and calls and chatter. We fronted up to the house at about 9.30, and were shown to our accommodation. Having lived in South Africa, I knew a rondavel as a round hut made of mud with, usually, a straw roof. This was round, but there the similarity ended. The walls were made of shadecloth strung around poles set in a raised circular concrete pad, the structure topped with a blue tin cone-shaped roof. One quarter of the inside was partitioned as the ensuite, with toilet, basin and shower. And frog! Three legs clung to the tiles near the taps, and one leg drooped dismally. It didn't move for the whole day and night we were there.

The room held a double and two single beds, a wardrobe and a chest of drawers, as well as a small glass-topped table and two chairs. And there was plenty of space to hold a party if we felt like it.

We didn't. Our intention had been to explore the wonders of the area as stated in the brochure - gorges, waterfalls, rock pools, all within driving distance in a 4x4. Unfortunately, the tracks were impassable even by the most robust of vehicles, let alone our little Rav4. Perhaps it was just as well.

After the rigours of the day before, and having had almost no sleep because his mattress lost its air, Barry was wiped out, and my body was still fighting the effects of a chest infection and attack by antibiotics. We spent the whole day resting and recuperating.

Unlike the camping ground, the area where the rondavels (there were three) were situated was quite heavily wooded. Well-protected from the sun, with shadecloth walls allowing penetration by any stray breeze, our comfortable abode was the perfect place to relax, sleep and dream.

Not that it was cool, although a ceiling fan kept the hot air moving. While Barry slept, I lay in a stupor for a lot of the day, unwilling to make a noise and disturb him but also too weary, perhaps mesmerised, to be bothered. It felt like we were the only people on earth, living in a zoo where we were the animals, caged in the middle of a forest that teamed with winged life.

Each specie takes its turn to call, roam its territory,

check for food. A noisy creature raps out its presence like an imperious knock on the door; a sports rattle - black and white - flits from twig to frond, darts under the eaves to pluck a spider that wasn't there yesterday; a couple of screeching parrots fly over; and never silent are the tweeters and chirpers. A blowfly checks the perimeter, bumping against the shadecloth in its attempts to join us. No other sound intrudes until an inquisitive breeze begins a search through the leaf canopy, touches, brushes, shakes, growing louder as it approaches. Dry leaves succumb to its probing, and there is a gentle patter as they fall all around our enclosure, while the breeze continues its search into the distance. Stealthy, measured steps throw my alert signal into orange. Are we not the only ones after all? Fear turns to delight as a bunch of peacocks plods into view, one of them an albino.

At about 3 o'clock we took the short walk to Paradise Pool. There must have been a reason for the name at one time but we found no evidence of paradise in the dry overgrown place so named. We followed a path of a kind, over rocky terrain, through scrub and prickles and blackjacks that caught in our clothes and my socks. It brought back forgotten memories of my childhood where blackjacks seemed as much at home in my socks as my feet.

Next morning, we were away by 8.30. Discussion about it the previous night had caused Barry some concern about crossing the Durack River, not to mention having to negotiate the track back to the Gibb River Road. In the event, the grader had reached the station by the time we left, and the road out was quite respectable.

Pat Fletcher

Auschwitz

The tour bus pulls to a halt.
Heavy with silence, we walk,
are not separated, women from the men,
ordered to strip, yet stand exposed,
frozen, in front of glass viewing rooms.

Tossed, atop one another,
victim's clothes, tailored, shop bought,
stitched by women around kitchen tables,
share the same fate.

Spectacles,
never seeing what was to come,
now bear witness.

Shoes, once worn by these souls
never again to feel soft grass, dance
to music of their homeland.

Zyklon B gas canisters piled high,
suffocate. I push one foot before the other.
Guide's voice, a whispered thread,
unable to drown shouts, screams,
reverberating along the chamber walls,
I wipe tears, free to walk through the gate.
but the images remain.

Marlene Fulcher

My Island Trees
Rottnest

Here it seems that nature
has spared nothing to render
this Isle delightful above all
other Islands I did ever see
from the log of
Captaim Willem De Vlaming
1696 - 97

My Island trees sing
dance, twist, bend
to call of wind
echo of waves
against my rocks.

Mankind settles – *Hale,*
Nairne Clarke and *Spyers,*
the resolute *Robert Thomson,*
Caroline, their eleven children,
stays my trees
midpoint the dance
curled and coiled
clinging to mother earth
tremulous, waiting.

August Seventeen
Eighteen hundred and thirty-eight
Corporals *Welch* and *Fulcher,*
Gee Esq,
initiate my darkest history
Ninety-three years
felled trees
lashes and heavy irons
shatter the silence

New vibrations echo
additional dwellings, Hotel
Visitors, who come
 to laugh and play
 under the sun

Once more my trees sing
listen to their rustle talk
tales of aeons past – know
deep within my soil
the magic lives.

Marlene Fulcher

A Childhood Niche

Coolgardie! The ghosts of childhood memories linger in its red dust, scorching summers, and brittle cold winters. Once a place of crows, peppercorn trees, tin fences, and abandoned mine shafts, years later, my mind still bears the imprint of those distant days of wonderful freedom.

I was five years old when we departed Northam, en route to an alien Goldfield's town. A raft of relatives and friends waved us goodbye as we journeyed east into the unknown.

After what seemed an eternity we arrived at Coolgardie and drove down Bayley Street, wide as two roads put together. The Railway and the Denver City hotels kept each other company on one side of the main street. We passed a picture theatre, a drapery store, an ice cream parlour, a police station, and a shire building, before chugging up and over a hill to a small house at 1 King Street.

Built by my Dad with asbestos and weatherboard, it was topped with a corrugated tin roof and surrounded by a veranda. Inside the kitchen sported a black Metter's stove, a kitchenette, a table and four rickety wooden chairs. Two basins perched on a cupboard served as a sink. In the bathroom resided a chip heater, a bath and little else.

A large tin dunny, a prominent feature in the back yard and a considerable distance from the house, resided under a giant peppercorn tree. It was serviced by a 'Night Cart Man.' Why he was called a night man was a mystery as he only ever visited during the day, a source of concern if you were seated atop the throne.

A hasty, inconvenient retreat ensued on hearing his rattly cart approaching. My first day in Coolgardie, I sat on the toilet's wooden seat, the door wide open, and surveyed my new surroundings.

This strange territory soon became familiar. Our King Street neighbours proved friendly and helpful and over time became our extended family. These days I occasionally forget names, but our Coolgardie neighbours are printed indelibly on the background of my mind: The Cramptons, the Cassidys, the Powels, the Purchases, the Purdys and the Lefroys. A kaleidoscope of images tumble over one another as I recall their names.

Out of school, life became an adventure of unlimited freedom of movement. Our skinny bodies obeyed every whim, climbing, cycling, running, and swimming. Feral children, the bushland and the slime dumps were our playground. Brown as berries, bare foot most of the time, the soles of our feet so thick we could walk through prickle patches without an 'ooh' or an 'ouch.'

Our favourite haunts were the reservoir, where we climbed trees to watch the brumbies thunder by, Paddy's dam where we dived for discarded cans on its murky bottom, and The Bluff, a huge outcrop of rock providing sanctuary for feral goats. Dotted with caves and tunnels, it was a young explorer's delight.

Always hungry, we satisfied our ravenous appetites, by raiding old Griff's mulberry tree, plucking grapes and passion fruit from vines hanging over fences and pinching pomegranates from unattended yards.

Another Coolgardie novelty was our huge backyard. It provided plenty of space for a chook pen, a fenced in vegetable patch and any pets who might stop by, and many did over the years.

Goolie Goat wandered in one day, looking for his mum and bleating plaintively. Showered with food and affection he grew into an impressive Billy goat who guarded the yard with a vengeance.

One day, when the front gate was left open, he spotted the postman approaching. Goolie locked onto him like a missile and charged, knocking him off his bike, ripping his trousers and scattering mail along the footpath. Luckily, the poor fellow didn't sustain injuries, and his shock abated after Mum administered a hot cup of tea. He was accustomed to unfriendly dogs, but never before been attacked by a feral goat.

Bill, a pink and grey galah, rescued after falling from a nest and spoon fed with porridge, proved a willing pupil when he matured. I'd taken to playing pretend teacher and the outside chimney provided an ideal blackboard. I gave my lessons, banging the chimney every now and again with my chalk for emphasis, while Bill jigged up and down on the fence squawking his approval. No doubt the neighbours were mightily entertained.

Stray cats in abundance reproduced at an alarming rate under our house and kept my mother busy drowning their kittens in the copper. Thankfully, she carried out these awful deeds while I was at school, and saved me, a sensitive child, from many a nightmare.

Dad built a hutch for a male and two female white angora rabbits. Cuddled and tamed they roamed the yard during the day and returned to their hutch for their evening meal. Ignorant of rabbit habits, when a great kerfuffle broke out in the hutch, I crawled in to find the cause. One of the females had delivered kittens and the buck was tossing them all over the cage. I grabbed him by the scruff of the neck and dragged him, kicking, and struggling to an old bird cage, and managed to deposit him inside, sustaining some nasty scratches in the process. I wondered how a cute, cuddly animal could be so nasty.

I'd always wanted a dog and when Dad came home one day with Toby, part dog, part dingo, I couldn't believe my luck. Admittedly he was no oil painting, but he was a dog and that's all

I cared about. Infested with fleas, his ribs stuck out grotesquely, and his matted coat indicated mange. Mum, no animal lover, objected strongly to the scrawny newcomer. "Take him back to the gutter where he belongs," she berated Dad. However, four against one, my sister, brother, Dad and I, sided against her and saved Toby's day.

We'd met with the same opposition against Goolie. Mum didn't like goats either, and to be honest, you couldn't blame her. If anyone committed the crime of leaving the back gate open, passing wild goats would troop in on washing day, and eat the clothes off the line. Buttons strewed the ground and half eaten skirts flapped in the breeze. Enraged, Mum would chase them, straw broom held high, emitting war whoops.

Mum proved a fierce opponent when her ire was raised. However, despite her objections, dog Toby found a home that day. Well fed, treated for the mange and fleas, he turned into a fine specimen. Highly intelligent, he possessed a lovely nature. He and I became great mates, and unbeknown to Mum, he slept on the end of my veranda bed and proved a great comfort on my 'down days.'

Not far from our home, up and over the Hunt Street Hill, stood the quaint Coolgardie State School. A rectangular building of rough stone, with a corrugated iron roof and surrounding verandas, it featured large double windows. A huge rainwater tank in the playground provided fresh water, and we drank from cupped hands held under the running taps.

Inside the building seven classrooms stood around a large hall. Here we learnt dancing and I vaguely recall a dancing partner named Brian. Perhaps we learnt sewing there too because when I reflect on it, images of hessian bag material, a gigantic needle and long stitches of thick colourful wool come to mind

Miss Allandale, Miss Henderson, and Mr. Caw are the only teachers I remember. They were short of teachers after the war and married women could return to their teaching careers if they reverted to their maiden names.

Miss Allandale, married with six children of her own, didn't stand for any nonsense. She also abhorred spelling or arithmetic mistakes. Dare to make one and a sharp crack across the knuckles reminded you to practise more diligence in the future. As small children we mightily feared her punishing stick.

Miss Henderson, a single woman, young, pretty, and caring must have favoured me. "Robin fascinates me," she told my mother. My classmates took angst at the favouritism and taunted me for weeks with, "Miss Henderson's little pet." Much as I liked her, she caused ridicule and ostracism to come my way.

Mr. Caw taught us in years six and seven or tried to. I never saw him wear anything but a black, shiny suit that clashed with his sallow skin. From what I can recall, he migrated from another country, and I don't think I ever saw him smile. I realise now he was probably a lonely man and would have struggled understanding the feral mob of children who confronted him each weekday.

I think he had a love for mathematics but failed to impart any liking for them to his unappreciative students. Every week we failed our math's test and were detained after school to get them right. After a day of lessons, even half an hour longer seemed endless, and we could no more concentrate on his mathematical equations spread out on the blackboard than circumvent the moon.

The excuse of having to go to the butchers, because he closed at four o'clock, sometimes worked but couldn't be used too often. Chappy Jones tried it three times in a row and was refused on the third request. 'I'm bloody goin' anyway," he yelled at Mr. Caw who promptly got out his cane. Dodging and jumping, Chappy managed to escape out the door.

The last we saw of him, glimpsed through the window, he

was furiously peddling his bike down the hill, hightailing it to freedom. Mrs. Jones, a war widow, was seen in the headmaster's office the next day. She brooked no interference where her two sons, Chappy and Ron, were concerned and was a tiger in their defence.

The day I left Coolgardie Primary School marked the end of my carefree existence. Secondary school loomed on the horizon, and the twenty-five-mile trip to Kalgoorlie five days a week to attend high school, left little time to roam the countryside.

Many years later I revisited Coolgardie. To my deep disappointment the house that Dad built no longer stood at 1 King Street. Only the dilapidated dunny, listing drunkenly to one side, still sat under the peppercorn tree on the now vacant block. The Bluff, the school, and the dam appeared much smaller than I remembered.

My childhood place vanished, I preferred to recapture the old Coolgardie, the Coolgardie of my youth, a precious time and place in the Goldfield's sun. Never to be forgotten, I've tucked its memories safely away on the back shelf of my mind.

Robin Giraudo

Toad

The relentless rain pelted down, as it had most of the day. The wind whistled around our ears as we continued to pack the small, reliable truck on the slippery, muddy driveway. The ground smelt disgusting as it always does at the start of the first winter rains. So much dog piss around, its sour smell rises and burns your nostrils as it makes its way to the back of your throat.

When the rain pelts down everything slips and slides in all directions and becomes one huge mud pit. Earlier, Alan had laid a tarpaulin down on the truck tray, not realising the edges hung over the sides. When he jumped on to the back of the tray, he slipped on one of the overhangs and, though he tried to save himself from falling off the truck onto the galvanised fence, he fell hard, sliced his arm, and blood gushed in all directions. Kalgoorlie is known for its old rusty fences: they are part of its heritage; been part of Kalgoorlie's landscape since the early Goldrush days along with their famous Hay street brothels.

The day had been long and tiring but finally we locked the front door behind us for the very last time; jumped onto the front seat of the truck. Alan turned the ignition and flattened the pedal to the floor as she creaked and rumbled getting into gear. Turning my head, I glanced back as Alan moved towards the highway.

In this mining town six hundred kilometres from Perth, Western Australia, a town with hotels on every corner, and of course the galvanised fences, in the midst of summer, you can smell the heat in the air on those long hot summer days, but not right now as rain continued to pour and wind gathered momentum.

Lisa and Deanna stayed in our caravan parked at a friend's place. Deanna, our eldest daughter, had started a new job in an accounting firm, and was comfortable in her new position.

Lisa, our middle daughter, was in year twelve; she had a boyfriend and a great circle of friends at school. They had no intentions of leaving Kalgoorlie. Alan and myself had already signed the documents so there was no turning back.

We bought a roadhouse, Yellowdine, which is located 402 kilometres east of Perth, on the Great Eastern Highway. It was originally a railway siding on the Southern Cross to Coolgardie line for the steam trains that had started running in 1896.The first prospector to discover gold in this area, in 1934, was Augustus Palmer, from Southern Cross, this following the main gold discoveries in the 1800s in Kalgoorlie and Coolgardie.

Life for the prospectors in those early days was harsh, the heat overwhelming, with infestations of flies and other pests, and a short supply of water caused many men to perish. This followed by bitter cold winters. Surrounded by mud and slush, they huddled in their small tents for relief and comfort away from the heavy rains, as the wind howled and whistled fiercely trying to destroy everything in its path.

In the early days, "Yellowdine" was known as "yellowdime," prospectors before the turn of the century finding a gold dime when starting to search for gold. This was much to everyone's disbelief for no one had travelled this far from Kalgoorlie.

Coolgardie's gold is richly coloured, beautiful, bright yellow, breathtaking nuggets, just like in the jewellers. The nuggets are in natural form – from the ground to the buyer – always if the weight permits, the value is the gold price of the day. Chryelised gold is in a completely different form – one would think it's been crafted with a knife. It's worth, in most cases, is higher than the gold price of the day, and is highly sought after in America.

Kalgoorlie and Coolgardie still are operating today. As the years passed, "Yellowdime" was renamed "Yellowdine", and remains so to this day.

This was our new destination: "Yellowdine Roadhouse".

Driving at quite a slow pace down the highway, the rain poured heavily on the windscreen making it difficult to see clearly. It was close to dusk. The kangaroos would be out and, where there was one, ten more would be close by. Groundcovers and small shrubs forced their way through the flat, sparse, red Goldfield's dirt and gravel, clinging to everything to survive. Way off in the distance we could see the lights of "Yellowdine". They appeared to flicker but we realised the road gave us a false sense awareness, and we must not become complacent. There was still sixty-five kilometres of straight road to travel.

At last we arrived. Jumping from the truck, Alan and I stretched and stared at the Roadhouse, thinking 'what have we done?' The place was huge and new. Then my eyes glanced further, past the bowsers to the accommodation sign leaning on a forty-five-degree angle. 'How long has it been like that?' I asked myself. 'Did nobody notice, or even care?'

No unpacking tonight. I couldn't wait to have a hot shower, followed by a delicious meal then crawl into bed.

As they turned in from the highway, trucks rumbled on the gravel surface, straight to the parking bay. Dust swirled and gathered momentum as they turned and reversed back and forth. The noise was deafening. I glanced at my watch: it was 5.00 am. Excited to hear so much activity outside – screeching brakes flat to the floor brought trucks to a screaming halt – drivers in a hurry for breakfast – a warm smile crossed my lips. Loud chatting, as feet stamped and dragged on the gravel as the drivers walked around the bottom corner of the roadhouse towards the dining room entrance. Chatter vaporised. Two refrigerated trucks parked side by side was the only sound to break that silence. I peered through the window curtain. A Kenworth had stopped at the fast flow a short distance from the bedroom – Fastflow was two hundred or more litres of diesel. Because of the volume, it was more cost effective for the driver.

Alan and myself slept peacefully.

Ray, along with his wife and family, joined us in this adventure. Jason is a strapping young man, large frame, big heart, usually wearing a bandana. He talked the talk along with his image. Jason was a gentle giant amongst men.

Toad was also joining us with his son, Daniel. Driving from Kew in the Northern Territory to Western Australia would be a challenge – though he has never shied away from a challenge – along with his old, battered, white rust-riddled Holden Station wagon. This car would bring a tear to any die-hard Holden man.

While in Kew, he worked in a laboratory: gold extraction. Prior to that he'd worked underground at Nepean gold mine in Coolgardie, Western Australia, in the early 1980's; had settled in Coolgardie with his wife and young son Daniel, who was the joy of his life.

We were settled in Perth at that time, along with Ray and Rae. We'd loaded up our cars, food, kids and beer, driving on the highway heading straight towards Coolgardie. Four hundred and fifty kilometres of road.

Toad was not a good gardener. He decided to have a clean-up, front and back of his property. Growth climbed up the stumps of his modest weatherboard home, also made an effort to attach itself around the beautiful huge peppercorn tree.

We finally arrived. Kids screamed with excitement as they scrambled and tumbled from the car.

Toad greets us with a warm smile followed with an ice-cold beer that dribbled down the side of his glass as he walked towards us. We made ourselves comfortable on the front step. We chatted and laughed idle hours away late into the afternoon. Kids ran crazy on the dry gravel path that extended to a small front gate which squeaked every time you pushed it open. Even if the breeze caught it and prised it ajar it continued to squeak. My eyes glanced at the stumps of this small weatherboard home, also the beautiful peppercorn tree.

"Toad, your gardening skills have improved."

"Wow! Amazing. Totally impressed," We both shook our head.

"I feel the homestead has character now, Bob," he replied with a grin.

"You burnt everything with the blow torch – even the stumps of the house are burnt … and the beautiful peppercorn tree."

"Well, Bob, it cleaned up pretty damn good. I am a happy man."

We all roared with laughter as he replied," No mowing for this guy."

It was a weekend to remember.

Focusing on addressing our meeting, followed by the grand tour of Yellowdine, we all stared in disbelief; gazed in horror at the hygiene of this kitchen. Fridges were mouldy along the inside of every door; the smell of mouldy, slimy, old withering vegetables. This kitchen was a disgrace.

Even though the building was new, everything in the kitchen was very old and dated.

This was disgusting! We looked at each other in disbelief. Why?

'Do these people have no idea or even care?' we all asked ourselves. 'Do the health inspectors never check these eateries beyond the metropolitan area?'

Moving towards the deep fryer, once again staring in disbelief, the cooking oil resembled tar that is used on the roadways for repair. Pitch black with a strong odour of aging. Burnt food bits floating on the surface. 'How is this possible in this day and age?'

Our decision was unanimous concerning the staff. Ray was our spokesperson. Approaching 11.00 am, the staff started drifting in one by one. Surely these young people must be aware of our decision. Ray, speaking in his business voice, addressed the group. They obviously had not a clue arriving at the meeting in such a scruffy state. Had they no self-respect at all.

Ray continued: "Bad habits cannot be broken. We no longer need your future services as we prepare towards a new profile and image for our dining room. Thank you for your patience – please be packed and ready to leave before nightfall."

One by one the drivers picked them up. Still waving as the last person left, holding my hand across my forehead as the rain continued to drizzle down on my face, the last truck drove out of sight. The only vision in front of me was the wet highway glistening black and endless as far as the eye could see.

Cloud coverage lingered like a blanket covering the sky.

Feeling a strange presence, I glanced towards the falling down accommodation sign on my right. Tucked behind a small shrub was beautiful Clancy, eyes fixed on the highway. Breaking his stance as he wagged his tail, he walked towards me, his head lifted slowly as if to ask, "Are you my new bestie now?"

Clancy was a Red Kelpie, known as the Yellowdine dog. Why these animals appear to have a strong pull towards isolated areas, well, I really do not know, but he won our hearts forever. He was an amazing animal as his gaze did not divert from the highway. Thinking to myself, why would someone leave this beloved animal behind? Nevertheless, everyone loved him, even the drivers. These animals are amazing working dogs, not to mention being a social butterfly. He was one of the team.

Damian, who drives a Kenworth, bought me in a photo of the old original broken-down Roadhouse twelve months later, as I previously asked. The photo was taken a few years prior to the new one being built. Guess who is standing right in the front with a huge smile … yes, you guessed it … it was Clancy.

Excitement buzzed around the kitchen as we continued to organise our special menu. This was our first party booking, a birthday celebration, in total four customers. Our guests were offered a complementary glass of port for their celebration.

Allocating different jobs between us, we started to prepare the evening special for the truckies – Shepherd's Pie with heaps of buttered mash potato. Old school recipes were a huge hit. Especially Roo-dog. The smell lingered through the kitchen and dining room. Delicious beef frying with onion; great base for the gravy. Potatoes boiling softly. Season, add meat and onion to baking dish, cook for a few hours. Prepare fresh vegetables then we are done.

I glanced across the room as Toad was preparing a tub of onion – it is a huge tub so we all take it in turns doing this unpleasant job. As I continued to walk across the kitchen floor, he turned and looked up. Fixed very firmly on his face were swimming goggles – bright green swimming goggles. He mumbled to himself, then blurted out: "Keeps the sting from my eyes. Maybe you should try it." I laughed as I continued to walk.

Ray and Rae were busy organising the Lime and Chicken kebabs for the party booking. This was a great choice for the entrée. They looked amazing, all perfect in size. Moving on to their main, presentation was everything. These guys were a good team.

Early afternoon as the phone started to run off the hook, the party booking had grown out of proportion, changing constantly. The softly spoken woman announced there would be thirty-five people arriving in total. "We were all very excited about our complementary port at the bar," she continued to add. "It is wonderful because we have a small bus, with allocated driver."

Alan was busy working the front counter while Jason worked the driveway.

"Staff meeting, now," Ray announced.

We all froze as Ray bought to our attention the 'complementary port'. For thirty-five people.

"Thirty-five!" we gushed, not to mention the extra preparation. But I guess the preparation was really not a huge concern, nor rearranging the dining room.

But the complementary port was a problem.

"Galway Pipe will not be on the bar. I'm sure we can come to a solution." Then Ray had a brilliant idea … "We still provide the port but not as originally planned," he continued. "Everyone knows that good port clings to the side of the glass …"

Alan jumped straight in the car, heading towards the bottle shops in Southern cross. "Two flagons of port please." He jumped back in the car and returned to the roadhouse.

Alan rushed in with the port. Ray heated the honey in the microwave then continued to mix it in with the port. We all stared in amazement, ready for the taste test; we gave it a swirl, it clung beautifully to the side of the glass. It was pretty good and yes it would pass the taste test.

Dining room ready – meals and all preparation complete – truckies' section ready. We are all at our stations, excited and nervous all at the same time. Our party guests started drifting in heading towards the bar. As we walked around with our clay carafes pouring the guests a port, people were quite eager to enquire about our fine port. It became a strong topic of conversation between the men. Of course, we disclosed, it came from a fine winery that specialised in this particular product. It caters only to licensed restaurants.

Our evening came to an end, all guests laughing and chatting as they jumped on their small bus to return home. We locked the dining room door then turned all outside lights off.

Ray had our glasses on the bar to celebrate – port of course.

On another night, all the truckers said goodnight as they left the dining room; scuffled towards their rigs for a good night's sleep. Alan and I had almost finished our work in the kitchen, though it was only 11.30 pm, not yet closing time. Picking up the empty milk crate as I walked outside, my favorite resting place to have a cigarette, I thought … *Our German travellers are happy inside chatting.* I call them 'bikers' because even though their number count was 15, these gentlemen were not rough and tumble like the "bikies" as we have experienced in the past.

Alan made his way to the office to finish the paperwork he was working on earlier in the day.

Such a still night with a soft breeze on my face, crisp and clean, peaceful and beautiful. Cigarette smoke vaporised as it swirled in all directions creates thought; my moment of isolation and solitude I treasure even though there is activity all around me. Times like this are rare and comforting, very limited but keep me sane as I collect my thoughts in private. The stars were overwhelming, twinkling, but as my gaze shifted there appeared to be more energy moving around the night sky – or was it just my broken train of thought? My gaze still lingered, staring, as I sat motionless.

One of our German travellers came over and asked, "What are you looking at?"

Toad also came over with his beer, "Hi, Bob, what's up?"

I turned to Ludwick and Toad, pausing for a moment, "If I'm not mistaken, those are the *Min Min*."

Noticing the lights hovering above, Toad nearly choked on his beer, then grinned from ear to ear, "*Min Min*? Really …?" he replied.

By this stage all our German travellers were sitting around wanting me to continue, as I explained how surprising it was for the lights to come this far across the border as they are only seen along the Northern Territory and Queensland border. Ludwick asked, "Well what exactly are they? Can we touch them?" His questions kept coming.

"Scientists believe the only explanation possible is combustion of gases. They are always in groups and cluster together bobbing up and down. One minute they will be in front of you then the next behind you. At times they appear to be close enough to touch but that of course has never happened."

Slim Dusty, the most respected country singer to come out of Australia, wrote about the *Min Min* lights in the early 1990's.

Our Aborigines' myth have their own interpretation on this phenomena: if a sacred burial site is desecrated, it releases a vengeful spirit to roam for all time.

We all glanced at the evening sky once more but to our surprise the lights had vanished.

Ludwick, and his friends were happy and said goodnight. Lighting up another cigarette, I sat firmly on the milk crate, and turned to Toad. He said, "Bob, you're full of shit, you know that."

I laughed. "Yeah, I know, but hey, it was a great yarn for them to take home."

We both laughed. The *Min Min* lights are very true but never in the west. Not ever.

Gazing at the stars I guess it was maybe just a dreamtime for me, lost in my own private space for just a brief moment. It was wonderful.

Picking up the milkcrate and smiling to myself, I went inside to finish my cleaning.

We are moving into 1991. The year the recession was starting to feel its presence.

And the highway died.

The coaches continued to call in for coffee and a chat even

though we were still not an allocated stop. Passengers would jump off the coach to freshen up, take a shower; some even had the cheek to fill their thermos then throw in a tea bag all at our expense, then quickly jump back on the coach thinking we hadn't noticed. We did not mind the drivers popping in for coffee, but we needed to do something about the passengers.

Ray had written so many letters asking the bus transport to consider our Roadhouse to be an allocated stop. It was rejected every time. At this stage, we desperately needed their support to survive. We were freehold.

Harsh times meant harsh measures. We put locks on all the outside showers and toilets – everyone had to pay. The following week coach drivers came in for coffee and all the passengers stayed on the coach. This continued for a further four months.

Truckies continued to support us, and even though it was a hard life, we still managed to have a laugh. On the odd occasion David and his pilot driver, Ted, shouted as they drank their coffee. David roared out to me as he turned his chair in my direction:

"Hey, Rob, I'm homesick," as he slapped his hand on his knee. "Sit on my lap and start whinging."

There was a roar of laughter through the dining room. As he continued, Roodog walked in with his off-sider. They looked buggered as they sat by the fire rubbing their hands together, and made small talk with David and Ted. Roodog was the most respected man on the highway.

We hired a young couple that were travelling around Australia, which worked well until Kerry complained bitterly about having to do so much cleaning. "Keep in mind," I said as I brought to her attention, "there is not one job I ask you to do that I do not do myself." Following that, I added, "If you don't like it, hit the highway with your resume … understand?"

We all spent Christmas together at Yellowdine that year. It was a happy time but not Christmas as we knew it. The table looked beautiful as it always had in the past. Bright coloured Christmas serviettes, gorgeous festive candles, and Christmas carols sweeping through the dining room. We all laughed and talked about everything and nothing.

The festive cheer died very quickly. All we could hear was a honking car horn. Shouting voices demanded service. I thought to myself, 'can these people not read?' The sign further along the highway said very clearly, CLOSED ON CHRISTMAS DAY.

We all drifted towards the pool area. The weather was beautiful not a single fluffy cloud in the sky. Chatting and laughing, pulling our sun hats over our ears as we sipped our beer. Hot summer lazy days by the pool … I shall remember that moment forever as I was so happy – we were all together, it was amazing. As we jumped into the crystal blue water, it swirled and glistened, the smell was crisp, hypnotic and soothing, as we made ripples with our hands on the surface, laughing and diving at the same time. Idle hours soon went by.

We all drifted into bed, and the girls returned to Kalgoorlie the following day. Geoff also had to return to the city. Little did any of us realise this was our last Christmas together.

Six months later, Ray, Rae, Jason and young Shannon left "Yellowdine" and returned to the Northern Territory as Ray was offered a partnership with previous work colleagues. They took beautiful Clancy with them.

Alan had his arm around me as we waved goodbye. Their car vanished out of sight as Clancy gazed out the back window. The sadness was suffocating I could hardly catch my breath as tears welled in my eyes. I asked myself, 'was it because they were leaving or was it because we were left standing on the driveway'. We all understood the place could not support three families but at the end of the day no one wanted to be here.

Ray mentioned when he was settled in his new business, he would send money for staff wages to replace them. As time passed it never materialised in the end, and we asked the question. His partners did not agree as the Roadhouse was none of their concern.

Alan, Toad and myself had some serious decisions to make. We were insolvent and still not making wages. Whether that would ever change we couldn't really say at that stage.

In the distant future as the years passed, Clancy was taken from us, a snake bite I believe. He was roughly fifteen years old. I guess that's a pretty good life, but it still hurt just the same.

Robyn Harrison

Home is my sanctuary

Home is my sanctuary
I'm surrounded by things that make me happy
Where I can be comfy and silly
And my dog makes me hairy
My bed is warm and cosy
And my bath is luxurious and soapy
It is my place of safety
I can hang out with friends and family
Over a coffee or a pot of tea
And if I'm in the mood, a glass of bubbly
Where I can stay in trackies
And have fun with my hobbies
Including bonsai, my tiny trees
To go with my love of all things Japanese
My kimono on display, with geta and obi,
And cook yummy food: udon, tonkatsu and sushi!
And not wear a bra or shoes and be free
My home: where I can just be
Despite my physical disability
Most of the time it's just my dog and me.

Melanie Hawkes

No Travel Required

Conversations, the TV, newspaper and internet are all filled with real-life drama. Almost everything is about COVID-19.

In our home we've felt it socially, financially and educationally. We've watched the economic forecasts, the number of cases and the ever-increasing death rate. We've heard about restrictions, social distancing and isolation measures. We've wondered.

Each time I've checked my emails, I've marvelled at how many mailing lists I seem to be on. Every company I've ever purchased from since the internet began has been in touch. They've reassured me they care about my wellbeing in these 'challenging', 'stressful' and 'uncertain' times, as we struggle towards a 'new normal'.

But this isn't normal. It's 'unprecedented'; history in the making. For me, things won't feel normal until I can enjoy a guilt-free hug.

I feel stuck at home, but I don't really want to step out into the world. It's easy to feel weighed down. Then I pause. Rays of pure gold seep into the seemingly bleak picture.

The sound of my children's laughter. Our clown-like dog who provides an endless source of cuddles and humour. Rediscovering the joy of puzzles (preferably puzzles that aren't fifteen shades of the same colour!). Being able to finish not just one book, but a whole series.

Time. To play cards and board games. To talk. To garden. To sit and do absolutely nothing. Not having to rush to kids' activities.

The knowledge that our house is small, but it's a house, not a confined European apartment. Having a backyard filled with tall, green trees, a riot of flowers and the sound of birds. The drop in traffic hurtling down our road. Our front yard being more peaceful.

Creativity. Resourcefulness.

The socially-distant chat with my neighbour from our respective front lawns. The circulating jokes that have me in fits of laughter as I sit in my little office. Discovering Skype and Zoom. The people I don't normally hear from who've reached out. The sense of community as everyone pitches in together.

Having a laptop that works.

Wearing the same clothes three days in a row. Not worrying about makeup or grey hairs. Living across the road from a local supermarket that saves me from big shopping centres. The camping box, which proved to be a treasure trove of cleaning products, hand sanitiser and soap. Discovering forgotten foods stashed in the pantry (best before dates are a general guide right?)

A sense of breathing space.

A good health system. The essential workers who've kept going, when they probably want to hole up at home. Living in a safe country, where political parties can put ideology to the side for a moment, and work together to focus on leading.

Being able to walk.

Feeling fresh air on my face. Watching the clouds and finding shapes in the sky with the kids. Blue skies. Autumn sunshine.

A sense of relief as social restrictions ease. The happy sound of our neighbours socialising again. Anticipation.

Guilt free hugs seem to be just around the corner.

Thank you, COVID-19. We didn't want you (and will be glad when you're done), but you've reconnected us with life's little luxuries. And they're right here in our home, no travel required.

Liz Hurst

Any Place

You stand
red dusty clothes piled high in arms too young,
skinny legs straddling cracked verandah boards
as you stare across a Namatjira scene
where orange, ochre, golds sprawl to horizon's shimmer
punctuated only by glistening ghost gums
and dead dry gullies.

You listen
as a young crow plays with its language
strives for perfection in the lingering stillness
as you pad to the pump
The tumult of water pounding into battered buckets
transports you to crystal clear pools
where you frolic near thrumbling cascades
tumbling down a distant gorge
the sound takes you to any place but here.

You trip
barefoot to the copper
each muddy splatter conjures cloud filled skies
damp nardhu fields
and fat sleek brown cattle
as you plunge dusty moleskins, denim blue shirts,
bandanas

scrub until the froth turns red,
the water liquid mud
then you dunk with disillusionment

Under an angry sun
you hang half people shapes
go back inside to burgeon your dreams with far distant places
places Grandpa painted in words
while you studied his face for the truth
but his face is like a roadmap of the places he's been,
each deep crevice swelling your mind with grand possibilities.

Outside the windmill sings –
like Dame Nellie Melba, grandpa says –
and you rush in desperation
shriek as a red cloud pirouettes the garden
jigs with faded moleskins;
jives with lazy shirt sleeves
waltzes along the fence that rolls forever.
Its howl bids you follow
invites you to places you've dreamt of
– to London
where ladies dress in fine lace and feathers
walk on needle heels

drink tea with elevated pinkies
talk in rounded vowels you sometimes practise.

Jostled by the wind swirl the crow flies off to a ghost gum
as you tear down your efforts
stomp inside and sweep the paddock from the table
fold red dusty clothes –
as you wish for black cockatoo skies,
a screeching Nellie Melba
mud pouring from the roof top
flooded nardhu fields
and market fat brown cattle
But all you hear is the mournful *Aaaaaah* from a treetop
And know it's the sound of lonely

Helen Iles

In the King's Mansion

A pictorial exposé

Morning dawns bright and sunny. I arrive bright and early at the ticket office on Elvis Presley Boulevard – well before the 9.00 am opening time – as do about two hundred other people who have lots to do in Memphis. A ticket to Graceland costs $34. Even though the purchasing of the ticket is speedy I am well back in the queue to catch the bus – yes, the bus! I can see Graceland across the road, but with Elvis Presley Boulevard being one of the main thoroughfares in Memphis it is too dangerous to walk across the six lanes of traffic to enter the grounds so a constant flow of shuttle buses line up under the pavilion and transport tourists across the road to the mansion's front door. A set of traffic lights from the souvenir centre controls the flow of buses. The trip also gives tour guides the chance to provide instructions and ensure the speaker-device for each person is working.

For $34 you get unlimited time in Elvis's house and can go round and round and round if you wish to satiate your Elvis appetite. The device provided is worn around the neck on a lanyard and by punching in numbers you get a running commentary of each room and facts about how Elvis used it. By punching in other numbers as instructed you can access further information about certain objects in the house should you want to learn more. And so, armed with this verbal encyclopaedia I board the 22-seater shuttle, thinking wholeheartedly "Di, I wish you were here." She had added Graceland to our planned trip driving across America, but had to drop out at the last minute, so I took the trip alone. Now, I briefly recall our regular outings as teenagers, watching the latest Elvis movie at the cinemas, or queueing for hours to see his diamond-encrusted gold Cadillacs at the Esplanade in Perth. Fans? Yeah, I guess you could say we are. "And, Di, this is for both of us."

As the bus starts to move my heartbeat races.

With not the slightest sense of urgency felt by all its passengers, the bus lurches slowly forward, brakes at the lights and waits for the six lanes of traffic to come to a halt. Then it casually dawdles across the road like a limping pedestrian; crawls through the gateway to allow all passengers time to view the tall black wrought iron gates with 'Graceland' embellished across them. Onto the bitumen driveway we shuffle along with the other buses – they move like a train – and wend around the curve amongst the vivid greens of manicured lawns, southern elm, crape myrtles and oak trees, to be deposited at the curved brown steps of the white columned, beige stone mansion.

My heart is thumping, rearing to go, but the attendant gathers the whole busload together and delivers the rules:

"Make sure your device is working. If it doesn't please approach one of the attendants, or come and see me cuz I'm your friend at Graceland. Make sure you press in the right number for the room you are viewing, otherwise the audio won't make no sense. You may take photos with your camera. But you must not take any video. Remember that, no video. Please, if a room is very crowded you can visit another room and come back to it. You can visit any room in any order. You can start at the back if you want and move your way back to the front here. Take as much time as you need to enjoy this beautiful home and to feel close to Elvis. Enjoy, everyone. When you're done, just return to the front here and hop on a bus back to the museums."

I climb the front steps to the white panelled doors, become one of the 650,000 or so visitors to Graceland each year, and move into the foyer.

The entry is dominated by a white staircase, the surrounding walls enhanced by Elvis portraits. A red cord prevents access to the stairway, and the guide advises: 'No one is permitted in the upper realms of the house. That was Elvis's rule back then, ensuring the privacy of his family and himself, and therefore that rule has been maintained since the house was opened and shared with the fans. Even Elvis's friends were barred from his private sanctuary.'

The front room to the right of the stairway is the lounge room, decorated in white and blue.

A set of stained-glass doors emblazoned with glorious peacocks set in gold borders to match the room beyond leads through to a drawing room where sits Elvis's piano, a place where Elvis can shut himself in seclusion to watch TV, sing for his own enjoyment, or compose.

It is very much a self-guided tour of look but do not touch – velvet cords draping across the doorways ensuring the rooms stay pristine.

I stay a long while here, imagining how the members of the family would behave in a room as formal as this, and listen to Elvis's music playing throughout the house. It's as if he is singing in the very next room and you'll turn a corner and he'll be there.

When the crowd in the foyer moves on, I turn and enter the hallway beside the staircase that leads to his parents' room, a room that has been unoccupied since Elvis's mother passed away. Tastefully decorated in whites and violets, which I believe was Elvis's mother's favourite colour, this room would have been Gladys's dream come true, coming from a small shack in Tupelo where Elvis was born. She now lived in a palace.

I move back to the foyer and into the formal dining room. The table is laid as if expecting Elvis to walk in for dinner. The audio device around my neck encourages me to consider the atmosphere of a full family gathering. Elvis and his friends however usually hung out in the kitchen and grabbed meals at all hours of the day and night.

Beyond the dining room lies the kitchen, a room of browns and golds that gives it a warm atmosphere. In this room Elvis and his friends would snack after midnight on his favourite fried peanut butter and banana sandwiches. The audio advises that this room was never empty – always someone in preparing meals or grabbing something to eat out of normal hours. It was the hub of most activities in the house.

Beyond the kitchen is the famous Jungle Room where Elvis would entertain, where his friends and the Jordaniares would erupt into impromptu singing late into the night. This room is famed for its Polynesian influence, with elaborately carved furniture, eccentric wood panelling and carpet on the ceiling, giving it the jungle canopy feel. At the end of the room is a feature wall that resembles a jungle waterfall. Elvis favoured this room as it reminded him of Hawaii, his favourite vacation spot.

Most intriguing about this room is the array of wooden, carved furniture, all highly polished and blending beautifully in with the greens and golds of the surrounding walls. Facing the back of the house this room received a lot of sun and drapes were nearly always drawn down or partially down, protecting the specially collected pieces of furniture, some superbly carved with animal heads. A stairway leads up to the private residence at one end of the room while another stairway near the kitchen leads down to the basement.

Further down the hallway and down a narrow flight of mirrored stairs is the basement TV room. Here, Elvis could watch five TV channels at the same time – he liked to stay abreast of the news – and spent much time listening to records and whiling away the time till his next movie, recording session or concert. On display are the old televisions and vinyl record collections of Elvis's favourite performers.

Through another doorway is the pool room, its walls and ceilings covered in gathered fabric, for what purpose I cannot fathom – unless it dulls the sound of pool balls dropping into the pockets, or stifles the noise of television or music in the next room. This room would be a nightmare to dust and maintain.

The rear of the house is simple, a vast expanse of lawn, a narrow, sheltered verandah and additional covered walkways leading to other buildings Elvis had built over the years.

I follow the crowd into the undercover gymnasium area towards the outbuilding, which may have once been a caretaker's house, but had been allocated as his father's office from where Vernon ran the business of managing Elvis's interests.

Graceland sits on 13.8 acres in the heart of Memphis. When Elvis purchased it however it was several miles from the Memphis townsite, the housing eventually building right up to its boundaries. The amount of land and location

protected Elvis somewhat from the intrusion of his fans.

The office area now houses a vast collection of Elvis portraits painted by artists around the world and sent to Graceland. Many of these portraits have at times hung on the walls of the home and are rotated through the establishment over a period of time.

Housed within the office block building is memorabilia of his birthplace and his time growing up, as well as an impromptu built rifle range where Elvis in his friends often practised shooting.

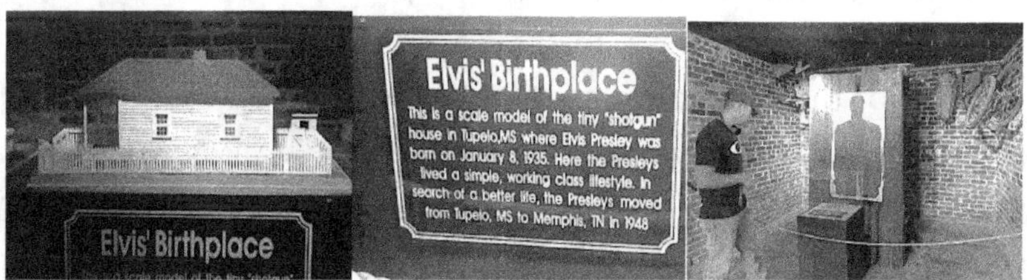

During his rise to fame and fortune, Elvis developed a love of horses and became a keen rider, eventually purchasing horses for all his family, and his friends. After his marriage to Priscilla, he brought her a stunning palomino called Rising Sun and, from that time on, the stable block at the bottom of the paddock was jokingly called "The House of the Rising Sun".

The various horses that lived out their lives at Graceland were always replaced with the closest possible replica in size, gender, breed and colour to always maintain as close as possible to how Graceland used to be.

So far on this tour I have seen the replica Rising Sun and a stunning chestnut, but not the Tennessee walking horse his father used to ride.

A small wooden sign at the edge of the lawn points towards and announces "Trophy Room". I head that way still listening to the pleasant commentary provided by my round-the-neck audio device.

I follow the crowd in through open doorways to the start of the trophy room, and trophy room is a great understatement. This *room* is actually a building, fitted out with display cases on the walls, the length and width of the huge hall divided into corridors by row after row of tall glass cabinets, each displaying the history of Elvis's career. I could spend a whole day here.

There are photos showing all the moods of Elvis, posters, costumes, records, and achievements that warranted a memory to be kept.

I walked the hallways, my memories stirred by the items on display, and a rekindling of the enjoyment I'd felt when I shared those moments Elvis had provided – record covers, some of which I still had at home – awards, and it came as a surprise that Elvis received a presidential award for his generosity and assistance to the community.

There were more paintings, a good many I would love to have smuggled home, and there were costumes from every movie he'd made.

The time ticks away and I become aware that I have plans for the afternoon, but every new corner brings further surprise and pleasure. I wish I'd not planned to fit in so much in Memphis on one day.

I move on. The Trophy Room exhausted, I return outside for further delights, follow another path to another building.

The sign outside says it is the Raquetball Building. He had his own squash court? Well, apparently he had, but it had been taken over as the Comeback Room and only a few areas of the lounge remain as a reminder of his time spent there with good friends, singing and rehearsing.

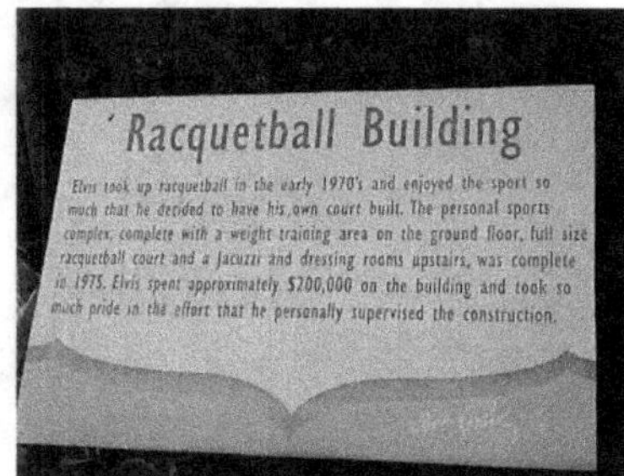

The Racquetball court itself had been converted into another trophy room – this time of the years of Elvis' modernisation of himself: wall to wall gold records and stunning costumes of his sellout tours. Awesome! But time is still ticking.

I'm on the move again, back outside, skirting the pool, imagining Elvis and his tight group lounging in the patio setting in the shade as I had seen on numerous TV documentaries.

It had happened right there.

I pass through the Meditation Garden and its tranquil peace. Tourists sit in silent contemplation, maybe feel closer to Elvis here in this place where he meditated and gathered his thoughts. And I soon realise the relevance of this stark feeling of solemnity. Beyond the garden is the small family cemetery, the final resting place for Minnie Mae, Elvis's grandmother, Gladys, his mother, Vernon, his father, Jesse, Elvis's twin brother who died at birth, and the King himself.

Tears were shed in this place even though decades have passed since his death and fans have travelled across the world to come to this place, to pay their respects and to mourn their loss.

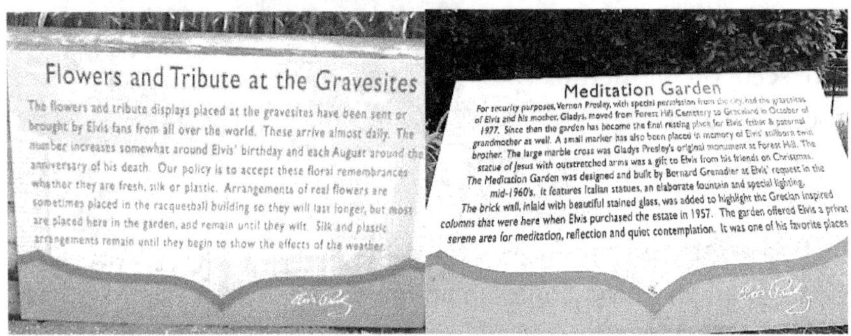

From here it is a short walk beside the Meditation Garden, back passed the beautiful well cared for horses, and onto the long grey drive that leads to the front of the house.

Here, as a last reminder of the diligence and regard of the Elvis Presley foundation, is a plaque acknowledging the gifts to Graceland, and a sign about the Meditation Garden.

And so, I leave Graceland, and board the bus for a much more lively 400 metre trip across the freeway to the souvenir shops. I could easily have spent a full day here and while I did not miss anything, it would have been nice to stay a while longer and remember so many good times when Elvis had been in my life.

So I settle back into my seat, appeasing myself that I will visit again on my next trip and slowly realise the one thing that has really peeved me off throughout the whole morning … there hadn't been once skerrick of dust anywhere! How do they do that?! A house that big … how do they do that!

Helen Iles

An extract from: Road Trip 1 – America or Bust

Kimberley Dream

To wake in my swag with a wide stretching yawn
and be gently caressed by a Kimberley dawn
in a camp that I pitched by a cold rippled stream
is only a part of my Kimberley dream.

White birds overhead that are bickering anew
wing far far away in the Kimberley blue,
to where cockatoos rest in Albizia trees
take my memories soaring on the Kimberley breeze
of crouched round a fire in a mustering camp
huddling to keep warm in the Kimberley damp;
of lying flat out on a pool crystal deep
soothing the skin in the Kimberley heat.
of droving the cattle across the vast plain
or cleansing the skin in the Kimberley rain
or when stepping to ground from a horse that I trust
to sink my feet deep in the Kimberley dust.

When I left this land long time my heart sorely hurt
till I lay my swag back in the Kimberley dirt
In the Kimberley sun or the Kimberley flood
the life in this land is my Kimberley blood.
And now in my swag watching black clouds form
I know it's the first of the Kimberley storms

The changes are coming, no seasonal regret
It's time for the winter – the Kimberley wet
When rainfall eradicates land's steamy haze
giving relief from hot Kimberley days
where far and wide such magnificence seen
rolls on and on in new Kimberley green.

After droving long years in this glorious land
I'll give my bones up to the Kimberley sand
To die in the top-end's a sure-fired must
so my soul can drift on in the Kimberley dust

And now that I've lived to life's journey's end
I let my soul fly on the Kimberley wind
I lie on my swag as life passes me by
'neath a boab tree 'neath a star-filled Kimberley sky

Helen Iles

Free Ohh

I forgot why I love you
until I smelt the sheep
shipwrecked on the docks
near the fallow rows of cars.
Until I sneezed when The Fremantle Doctor
tickled my nose with briny whiffs
of fish and chips
and the Cappuccino Strip.

We came of age in the eighties and shook
that ewer trophy at the world. Said
now that's a keel. King Alan Bond traded his trident
for the 'Auld Mug' and dared the Pollywogs[1]
to cross the equator and meet the Aussies.
We challenged them to beat us—down under—
on Gage Roads in our Freo. Hoisted the flag
of a boxing kangaroo with red gloves,
on the yardarm and taunted them—
Come on mate, have a go.
Come and play down Freo way.

---

[1] *Pollywogs are new sailors, especially one crossing the equator for the first time*

Shoaling and schooling we met
at the sailing clubs, Challenger Harbour,
on The Esplanade beneath green and gold
banners and bunting. We learnt to love
aboard South Terrace cafes. Newborn cosmopolitans
wiping coffee froth off our lips

like seasoned drinkers. Lived moored moments
in Papa Luigis' and Gino's before sailing
onto sidewalks where cruising hoons
in grumbling and rumbling cars
nudged us back to shore. Navigated
the flotsam[2] and jetsam[3] of socialites,
citizens and shoppers.

Voyaged through the hubble, jubble mayhem markets
of salty tourists gorging themselves
on twee souvenirs and pistachio gelato. We were adrift
on fair-weather streets filled with buskers and bag ladies,
and the Bhagwan's Rajneeshees.

---

[2] *Flotsam is floating wreckage of a ship or its cargo.*

[3] *Jetsam is part of a ship, its equipment, or its cargo that is purposely cast overboard or jettisoned to lighten the load in time of distress and is washed ashore.*

Steering ourselves by the streetlight stars we tacked
through becalmed streets from pub to busker
to pub. The Newport and Norfolk siren songs
called us to prostrate ourselves in polished brass bars
with boutique beers. Indulging ourselves
with summer sailors and drink and food and drink.

Drove to the festooned docks
or solitary South Mole—as wrapped up in ourselves
as Krishna clothing—listening to ships moaning
on their way to sea past Rottnest Island. Skimmed the marina
and gaffed our lagan[4] friends,
then swayed down the gangplank
of freshly-renovated heritage homes.

It was me who left you, who left for decades
each time. I always come back. You call to me
on The Doctor as it pushes to the bush.
I'm here to stay now, but
you're not the same. The lights are dimmer,
my people are gone. Facades are grimy,
and your one-way streets are bleak
and soiled with commuters.

---

[4] *Lagan (also called ligan) is goods or wreckage that is lying on the bottom of the ocean, sometimes marked by a buoy, which can be reclaimed*

Where are the buskers, bag ladies, and Rajneeshees?
Have they departed for new ports?
I still love you but
they took my Freo with them.

Kathleen Knight

The Silent Heroines

It is almost the end of the year. Our Arts and Crafts Club, which consists of a group of eight to ten grandparents who are the primary carers of their grandchildren, decide we should have our Christmas party before the kids' school summer holidays.

The decision to choose the venue for our Christmas party is made by each member of our group taking turns each year. As it happens, this year is my turn. I decide that we should go to a small local pub with a great outdoor BBQ area and a lot of shade among the olive trees. The garden is full of a variety of lovely greenery with flourishing flower beds and small scrubs where small birds usually nest and happily chirp while hopping around looking for food. I feel this place will be a perfect ambiance where we can farewell our old year.

A special lunch offer on the day includes a choice of a cocktail or a glass of wine. I arrive early to check our table is booked and ornamented with proper Christmas table decorations. For each lady of our group, I place a small surprise gift, which I made during the year with our Craft group, next to their plates. When the ladies arrive and make themselves comfortable, Jennifer, a tall and vigorous woman well past her middle age, is the first person to rush to the bar to order her special cocktail. She knows what she wants, giving other ladies advice on what to choose, describing each cocktail in detail. She is quite an expert.

"Jennifer, where on earth have you learned so much about the cocktails?" I ask.

"I was once a barmaid," she answers back with the most

charming smile. "I worked in pubs for most of my life. Now I am stuck with raising two grandkids that my daughter left behind. Who knows where she is now – probably getting drunk with her new boyfriend somewhere up north in some godforsaken pub. I haven't heard from her for ages, and I hope I don't see her any time soon because she is nothing but trouble," Jennifer says with an expression that betrays deep concern.

Wilma, a plump little lady in her early sixties, wearing an out of date dress with roses faded with age, gets up to join Jennifer at the bar to place her drink order. As she moves away from the table, Wilma waves her hand, calling us to follow her.

"Come on, girls, let's line up behind Jennifer. She will help us select the best choice."

A few minutes later, Wilma returns with her oversized fizzy drink, casually sits down with others, and starts sipping her appetizer, making a watery mess.

Then I ask, "Wilma, how are you managing with your grandchildren?"

"Not bad," she says. "Justin is doing really well at school, and next year he will be in high-school. I dread the school holidays as I have to let Justin go to New Zealand to see his dad. Christmas is not going to be the same without my Justin; I had him since his mother passed away when he was two years old. His father was in prison, and Justin hasn't seen him for years. Now that he is out, he wanted to see his son. Mind you, his father paid for his airfare. What can I say? He is Justin's dad, and he's got legal rights, but nobody bothered to ask if I was happy with that! Why should they, I am only the grandma."

After a collective sigh of consent, we all try to reassure Wilma not to worry too much because we are all faced with the similar predicament every day.

When everyone has ordered their lunch and made their

choice for the exotic cocktail, we all relax and start to chit-chat about small things, consciously trying to disengage from the troubles at home.

Another elderly lady, Valerie, tries to boast how smart she is with her finances.

"Look at me, what do you think of my sexy hair-do? Girls, this is going to save me money. This short-cut hair style will keep me away from the expensive hairdressers for quite a while. Isn't it good?"

"You look gorgeous, Valerie." Approvals come from all around.

"But why the purple colour?" I ask.

Valerie takes a seductive lady-like pose and says, "Why not? I want to be a cool granny, keep myself young-looking and trendy. Look, I even got a new tattoo on my ankle, isn't it super-cool?"

Valerie is always a joker, always so cheerful and happy. We all love her – she gets so chirpy when she has one or two extra drinks.

Then Olivia, the oldest in the group, tries to join the conversation. Olivia is close to seventy. Recently she's had a knee operation and is not so steady on her feet. She uses a walking stick for support, but that doesn't stop her; she is full of bubbles. Olivia starts in her slightly trembling but full voice. We all know she has trouble hearing, so we always have to hush her down a bit, not to talk so loud. In response, Olivia will giggle and try to be apologetic.

"Sorry, girls, I'm struggling with my hearing aid. I need a new one, but I can't afford it because Christmas is around the corner and the money I have I need for my grandkids that always come first."

Adjusting her seating a little with the help of her walking stick, Olivia continues.

"Last week I had trouble finding a reliable pest-control

company. I spotted a Redback spider's web on my washing line, and I'm worried about my teenage boys who like to play with their ball around and under it."

"Who did you call?" someone asks.

Olivia seems somewhat upset.

"I found one pest-control in the yellow pages, but when I gave them a call, I've got a bloody answering machine. I get so flustered when I have to talk to a machine, so without saying a word I just put my phone down. It's not like talking to a person, is it?"

No one disagrees. All sympathise with an old lady who, for fear of making mistakes, rejects digital technology altogether.

"Olivia, how many kids do you have in your care?" somebody asks.

In a calmer voice, Olivia resumes her narrative. "I have two boys since they were toddlers," says Olivia. "Their mother died from a drug overdose while their father, my irresponsible son, decided to work overseas, only to conveniently forget to come back home like his father Joe, who left me stranded to care for these two boys on my own. My ex-husband couldn't stand the noisy kids in the house, so he packed his bags, bought a one-way ticket to Thailand to meet his online dating chick, and never returned. Do I complain? No, at least no one bosses me around anymore."

I detect a tinge of sadness in Olivia's voice. For a moment, she looks somewhat dejected but quickly recovers. With renewed energy, she soon grows excited and is on a roll again.

"Yesterday that pest control company called back. Wow, that was a surprise. One girly-voice asked me if I still need their service. I could hardly hear what that girl was saying because the kids came from school and were making a lot of noise around the house. The girl on the phone sounded like some squeaky Asian from a mail-order bride service responding to my husband's inquiries. And, with my bad hearing, I understood only every other word of what that girl was telling me."

Some of the ladies around the table grin. Olivia starts to chuckle in anticipation of what she is about to say next.

"After some tussle, I finally realised that the girl was asking me something like, have I checked the *Web* for the information about the spiders. I told her again that I'm sure it's a Redback spider's web; there is no doubt about it, I don't have to recheck it – I'm not stupid. The girl hurriedly mumbled sorry, saying she doesn't understand what I mean. Then she said that I should use *the Net* and go *online* to get all the information about their pest control service. That's when I lost it. I told her that I've already taken all my clothes off the washing line because I'm not silly to leave any on it with the Redback around. And what am I supposed to do with the fishing net? Still, I got even more confused when that squeaky voice, which I could hardly understand, told me that I could *download* what I want from their *Website*."

Everyone around the table is suppressing a laugh, encouraging Olivia to continue with her story.

"Finally, the girl said that she'll send someone to check my washing line. Then she asked me about how will I pay the technician, and I said with cash. She said that cash is no good. I said, *Excuse me*! What's wrong with my money? She said nothing is wrong with my money, but they prefer *payment online* or a credit card because their business is going *cashless*. Now I was furious and flew off the handle. I told her that I don't have a credit card because all the cards went with my husband when he left me. And, since I have no credit rating, the bank won't issue me one. All I have is my miserable pension to support myself and my two boys, making me also bloody cashless. With that, I slammed the phone down."

The whole table burst into wild laughter.

Someone asks, "What happened with the spiders?"

Olivia rallies a little and answers decisively, "I went to Bunnings and bought insect killer surface spray and got rid of the Redbacks in five minutes; killed them all; they are all gone."

Now we laugh ourselves silly, clapping and applauding Olivia for her resourcefulness. Olivia joins in and seems in a buoyant mood not minding us making fun on her account. Of course, needless to say, Olivia isn't computer literate, and it isn't at all surprising that to her *Net* is for fishing, *Web* is for spiders and *Online* is for washing – a real 'dinosaur' when it comes to computers and the internet. But we love her because she is a lovely lady and doesn't mind if we sometimes have a laugh on her account. Indeed, she always joins in the group's uproar, telling us how lucky she is to belong to a bunch of such lovely ladies.

When the laughter subsides, Lesley, another likable elderly lady, jumps into the conversation with an outburst.

"Have you heard about how to download your kids' school reports? The school rang me last week advising me how to do it, but I was too embarrassed to admit that I don't have a computer or a printer. What am I going to do? Can someone help?"

Olivia giggles, "No good looking at me."

"I'll help you," responds Suzan. "When you're ready, come to my house, and we'll sort it all out."

Although recently retired, Suzan is still working part-time in HR for a large mining company. Before her retirement, Suzan assumed full responsibility for her two granddaughters, whose mother disappeared with a boyfriend. Computer savvy, Suzan always helps us if we have any IT or computer issues at home.

Lesley says *thank you* and indicates there is something else.

"I also asked, while on the phone, if I could purchase the books for my granddaughter's first year at high school, and that young girl casually said that I can find all the information on *Facebook*. I said I'm not on *Facebook* and asked why she couldn't simply tell me how to buy books in person. The girl then told me to place my order via the smartphone; it would only take a few minutes because it's simple. I told her I haven't got the smartphone, only the land-line, which is all I need. The girl at the other end went silent, so I asked again why can't I buy school books over the land-line phone, why this bureaucratic snag for ordering a few school books? Instead of an answer, that woman just put her phone down. I felt like taking my yellow *brick* phone off the wall and go to school and, with it, whack that insolent woman over the head. That would really teach her to show more respect to older people."

Still, Lesley finds that funny, and we all laugh with her.

She is right, I think. For some of us, the world is spinning too fast. It's run by young people who only worry not to miss out on anything in their life. As for grandparents like us, we suffer age bias as the most common form of prejudice in our youth-orientated society. Even worse, their children and grandchildren see older people marginalised as useless and surplus to requirements in the family. What the grandparents do for their grandchildren seems to be taken for granted and not appreciated by anyone, not their children, not their grandchildren, not by society and not by the government. You turn 65, and you'll be seen as a relic of the past – inconsequential. I shake my head to dispel the depressing thoughts. Let's not think about it now – today is too precious for that.

The party goes on for another hour. We all have a good time. Then I hear someone say, "What a lovely year it has been; let's hope that the next year will be just as good." One by one, we all get up and give each other a hug – a gesture of encouragement, love, and support.

"Ciao everyone," I wave as I exit the garden.

They all wave back. Looking at them for a moment longer, I see brave and spirited elderly ladies looking after their grandchildren in the world that doesn't appreciate them. Yet the world we live in is a much better place because they are in it.

I have no doubt, for me, these grandparents as carers are the *Silent Heroines*.

Nada Lubay

(Extract from *On the Wings of a Swan*)

Sunday Morning Coming Down

Entering the big brick building which houses the Gosnells Railway Markets, I am assailed by an explosion of sounds, smells and colours. To my right is a small stage, where a Johnny Cash look-alike is belting out a country and western song – something about being alone on a Sunday morning.

The deafening clatter of china and clanging of cutlery reaches me from the nearby international food hall, where people of all ages have congregated to enjoy a good chat over an unconventional breakfast of Asian food. Tempted by the tantalizing smells of Chinese, Indian and Thai cuisine, I head towards the Indian kiosk but am diverted by the irresistible aroma of freshly brewed coffee.

With a large flat white in my hand, I carry on towards the steam engine from which the markets take their name. The inscription on the side of this enormous engine, informs me that it was built in Great Britain in 1946 and was installed here when the markets opened in 1991. Two giggling teenage girls are having their photograph taken in front of the engine, and the popularity of this huge locomotive is evidenced by images of other young people smiling at me from a side display.

At the top of the first aisle, a Union Jack flag flies outside the *Candy Shop* and, approaching the entrance, understanding dawns, as the scent of long-forgotten treats immediately transports me back to my childhood and I leave with a little goody bag, my mouth watering in anticipation of the sweet delights ahead.

Continuing my tour, I pass stalls displaying jewellery, DVDs, shoes, mobile phones, carpets and clothing – even massage and hairdressing booths, but it's the sound of wind chimes and the perfume of cedarwood, emanating from a tiny New Age shop, that attracts my attention. Here, among the incense, candles and lucky stones, carved figures nestle together with images of fairies, witches and other mythical characters, all facing in the same direction, as if trying to escape from the tiny space afforded them in this mystical world of the magical and the mysterious. Pushing my way past the small queue of people patiently waiting to have their palms read, I discover the book corner and am soon immersed in the wonders of witchcraft and astrology.

Finally emerging from this fantasy land, the world outside the stall appears a little dull, until I notice the aptly named *Nick Nack* shop. Balanced precariously outside the tiny shop are gadgets ranging from banana slicers and button extenders to pegs and parsley cutters. I could stay all day but quickly tear myself away as I realise I've been here for two hours already.

Making a mental note to visit more often, I make my way to the exit, where, above the crash and chatter of the food hall, the sound of Sunday morning country is still coming down.

Val McCabe

Special Places

Special places infuse my soul.
They transform my heart from hollow to whole.
As I recognize that language or scent upon the wind.
I know my journey to this special place is about to begin.
I remember moments captured long ago.
In that far off place where we did go.
That restorative power of places that take you in.
Ones that release the valve that materialism sinks us in.
Shapeshifting our mindset that less is more.
That humans don't need to compare or keep score.
Yes, I've again found that place.
Now that I've given up the rat race.

Elizabeth Pappas

Summer's End

Drawing to a close a long summer's day.
I look over fields that once reaped golden hay.
Aloft a sky streaked like a ripe strawberry lush.
The earth sighs and relaxes into a contented blush.
Crickets sing as birds shelter in trees.
The temperature goes down by a few welcome degrees.
All thanks to an incoming sea breeze.
Rest gentle awhile with head reclined.
Enjoy the scent of rose blossoms and lemon rind.

Elizabeth Pappas

Tides of Childhood

A long seam of gold on a stretched-out summer's day.
Between two rocks on the smooth pebbled beach
the children play.
Extending the span of time when they must go back
To Pyrgi Palace, their parent's seaside shack.
Off the pier they run and then dive.
Into an ancient tide where dolphins thrive.
Splashing and swimming like fish in the Ionian Sea
The only thing that will shift them is a call for afternoon tea.
In these children's hearts
this escape from home is as precious as gold.
Forever in future dreams of childhood their hearts will hold
This place as if made of filigree nuggets manifold.
With the turn of a wave the passing of time will forever enfold.

Elizabeth Pappas

In My Backyard

Last winter my box tree by the kitchen window was severely cut back, only the trunk with several branches sticking out at the very top remained. I well knew that this would have been detrimental to birds, but it had to be done for it towered over the house, not a safe prospect considering the winter gales we are lately experiencing.

Not owning domestic pets my backyard is a haven for birds for there are trees and shrubs growing. A bowl of water constantly sits at the bottom of the box tree. Here they enjoy drinks and baths. Last year, when for some reason birds were many, at times there was more than one species vying with each other for a drink. On occasions, a few Willie Wagtails would socialise by the bowl taking turns to slosh in the water. Tail and wings flapping, water splashes all around. A pleasure to watch.

For a short period after the box tree had been ruthlessly pruned the number of birds dropped in my backyard. The box tree must have been their preferred hide out. How I missed them! I'm attracted to birds as I am to many other species of animals, I must point out though that snakes are not on the list. Their slithering bodies generate a sense of revulsion in me.

Not seeing birds using the bowl for several days I supposed that they wouldn't be around up to when the tree grew back, so I didn't bother to refill it. This was a wrong move. On the second day that the bowl wasn't refilled a Willie Wagtail landed by me as I was hanging the washing on the hoist. It stood there staring at me in a persistent manner. Willie Wagtails never stay put for long, they are consistently after insects moving about in the green lawn. I talked to it, I looked back at it several times as I kept on hanging the washing; it kept on looking at me insistently and wouldn't budge. Eventually it flew away. Its unusual behaviour made me think of the empty bowl by the tree. I promptly filled it up with fresh water. I couldn't believe my eyes when the following morning not one, but two Willie Wagtails happily swooped repeatedly in front of me as I was doing my daily chores in the garden. This gave me the most pleasant feeling of contentment.

Now that the box tree is thick with new shoots already two or three metres high, birds gradually are making a comeback. There are doves, magpies, Willie Wagtails, white-cheeked honeyeaters, singing honeyeaters and magpie larks. Every morning I make sure that there is enough water in the bowl to last through the day, on hot days they all make good use of it.

Silvana Preo

My Willie Wagtail

They like to nest in the broad box tree
my Willie Wagtails

when in the garden sipping my morning tea
one or two land close to me
they flutter about or eagerly rush to a meal
they never stay still

my backyard is their adopted domain
they chase off doves
with butcherbirds they might pick a fight
'off my territory' they clearly imply

they chirp and tweet when the time is right
they attend to their young with pride
if fresh water is not readily supplied
they've got a way to catch my eye

in summertime a playground
their bowl of water turns out to be
they bath and swoop and play about
taking turns with visiting friends

I take good care of my Willie Wagtails
They cheer my days like good mates

Silvana Preo

The Summer People

And then, while the lightning flashed outside, and the radio faded and sputtered, the two old people huddled together in their summer cottage and waited.

--Shirley Jackson "The Summer People" (1950)

There was no warning. The suddenness with which the fire swept through the bush, feasting on everything in its path, caught the authorities off guard. By the time they prepared to issue an evacuation notice, the fire had crested the knoll at the edge of town and was galloping towards them. Skipping over firebreaks as if they didn't exist, it gorged on oil-rich eucalypts.

Years of drought-stricken country offered fuel to the flames in obeisance – feeding them, growing them, making them harsher and hotter until they had coalesced into a ravenous, malevolent demon with its own weather system. The fire-demon consumed towns and tens of thousands of acres of land. It whirled and twisted and changed directions at a whim. It devoured houses, vehicles, animals and people, and spat out charred carcasses in its wake. Unhindered by the efforts of firefighters, unbothered by promised rain that never fell, it grew faster and angrier with each conquest.

They had prepared as best they could.

"The gas and electricity are off," he said.

"The bathtub's filled," she replied. "We'll be okay for drinking water."

"The windows? The doors?" he asked.

"Yes," she said. "I've hung wet towels and blankets on the

windows, and rolled them into logs for the base of the doors. Did you get the air-conditioner vents?"

The old man nodded. It had been a hurried job, but he had shut and sealed the vents with sticky tape and jagged pieces of the old styrofoam fishing esky he'd ripped apart.

"The car. Be quick," he said. She gave a short, sharp nod and drove their car into the garage.

She threw sodden blankets over the vehicle – the quilt her mother had made for her as a wedding gift, the wool blanket she'd knitted for their first child, the one who hadn't survived beyond a month – while the old man soaked the lawn and the roof and walls with the garden hose one last time. She slammed the garage door closed and gathered the pile of photographs she'd left on the dining table. In the fire-proof safe inside the wardrobe of their bedroom, she flung a hastily written letter to their children and the photos, on top of the title deeds for the cottage. Photos of them on their wedding day, smiling and laughing in sepia with hand-painted lips and eyes and hair. A black and white photo of them a few years later when he'd gotten a promotion, standing on the lawn outside this cottage, a large 'sold' sign planted into the grass next to them. The sign had been white with large red letters. They had both been so proud and happy. There were photos of their children too; tiny and beaming, dressed in Santa hats, as insouciant teens, and later, with children of their own. The photos marked her existence, claimed the space she displaced in the world.

They made their way to the kitchen – the most central room in the house – closing doors behind them as they went, determined not to give the fire-demon one breath more of oxygen than it could steal. It would have to wrest the air from their lungs. They would not surrender to it willingly.

The transistor radio, their constant companion over the last few days, their lifeline to the outside world, their only source of information and warning, breathed its last gasping breaths before falling silent. Outside, the bird calls and insect chirpings that usually punctuated their day had also hushed. An oppressive silence surrounded them, pressed heavily down on them, muffling even their own grunts and shuffles. They became self-conscious of every scraped foot, every gasped breath, every escaped whimper of fear.

They were completely alone now – isolated in a way they had never felt before in this remote seaside town. Despite the tyranny of distance, despite having to make do without the conveniences of everyday modern city life, despite having to break into the community of this small town and make friends, they had never felt bereft, as they did now.

The whoosh and roar, the crackling and snapping of kindling grew louder as the fire bore down the hill towards them. The apocalyptic, blood-red sky they woke to, gave way to a smoke so dense that no chink of light could penetrate. Their world was thrown into an inky midnight in the middle of the day, broken only by the flashes of lightning spewed by the fire-demon.

They huddled on the floor behind the breakfast bar.

"I'm scared," she said.

He drew her into his chest, and wrapped his thin body around her. She wondered when he had grown so frail, so old. She remembered reading about a couple found in the remains of Pompeii after the eruption of Mount Vesuvius. They had been entombed in ash and pumice, a perfect statue preserved for all time. They had been huddled together, the woman tucked into the man's chest just as she was tucked into his chest. She inhaled sharply, stifled a sob – she would not waste her final moments with tears. She was certain now that this was how death would claim them.

A short, muttered curse escaped her lips for all the words that remained unsaid between them, all the words they had run out of time to say, and she raised her face to him. He looked down at her, sensing her distress, and smiled. His face transformed into the man she had married 50 years before, the one with a cheeky glint in his eye, the face of a man who had been so sure of his future, of her answer, of their life together. Love and fealty, thanks and gratitude, passed between them in the charged air.

Asha Rajan

Down the Line

The ship docked at 8 am on a clear day in March. The flatness of the water in Fremantle Harbour, so different from the churning waves around Southampton that they had left behind several weeks before, took the immigrant passengers by surprise. Resisting the push and shove of the two hundred bodies jostling to get down the gangplank, the man and his son stayed close together. The boy's eyes were alight with excitement.

"How d'you like the look of that, Dad? Our new home!"

His father stiffened. "It's not the white cliffs of Dover, son. We're British. You can only ever call a place home if it's your mother country." And he held firmly to the boy's hand as they moved down the line.

The man, a motor mechanic, found work quickly. They rented a house nearby.

"Trying to give the boy a new start in life," he told his co-workers. "The wife died in 1974. She always wanted to move to Australia, better opportunities for the boy, she said, and he kept reminding me. Took us a year and here we are."

They were welcoming. The foreman invited them over to tea.

"Tea!" the man said mockingly to his son as they drove home. "And this barbie business, stuck out in the backyard! It's uncivilised! Not like our tea back home, properly laid up, tablecloth an' all. Ham's not the same neither, nor are the bangers."

"Snaggers, Dad," corrected the boy.

"Snaggers, my foot! You speak English, son, and remember

where you're from. It's a proud heritage, not like this mixed bag here. Descended from convicts mostly. Don't pick up their habits."

"But we're no-one special, Dad. We're Ten Pound Poms. Remember!"

His father stared at him. "Don't you let this lot label you, son. You're better than that."

"But Dad …"

"But nothing. Mind your manners and do as I say."

The man was pleased with the education system. "It's very British, seems like, so you'll have every opportunity to make a go of it. Work hard and you'll soon be laughing at the other fellers."

"I don't want to laugh at them, Dad. I want them to be my mates."

"What? *Mates*! You're picking up a lot of this slang stuff. I've told you about that before. You look around and find yourself some nice English lads. That's the way to go."

"But Dad…"

"Don't argue!" and the boy did as he was told.

One thing the father encouraged was togetherness with his son. "That's the way to keep them on the straight and narrow," he told his fellow workers. They smiled. It was something they already knew.

Fishing was a favourite occupation. The boy loved prawning and they bought a small, flat-bottomed boat so they could catch prawns and fat, blue crabs.

"The water's so clear," said the boy in wonder, peering over the edge of the small vessel. "It makes fishing more fun when you can see what's going on."

"It's all right," his father grunted, "but it's not a patch on trout fishing. You haven't really fished until you've tickled a trout. I used to do a lot of it back in the Old Country. In Staffordshire, it was. My boss took me during the season. He paid for it, of course.

Costs a lot, even for a weekend." And he talked on as the boy's eyes dulled and the crabs scurried by.

One day, when his father suggested an outing to the estuary, the boy turned away.

"No thanks, Dad. I've had enough of fishing." And that was that.

When the boy was nineteen, he met a girl from the country with dark, tangled hair and strong shoulders. She shared his love of outdoor life. He introduced her to his father, who nodded but didn't smile. Afterwards, his son sought him out.

"Dad, how could you treat her like that? You practically ignored her. You're the one who's always going on about good manners and look at you!"

"Watch it, son. You know I told you to find English friends. She's not one of us. She won't stick to you. She doesn't even wear proper shoes - only those flip flop things. What kind of upbringing has she had?"

The boy didn't answer but he started staying out later.

"Why don't you bring your friends back to the house?" asked the father petulantly.

"You wouldn't like them, Dad."

"Well, give me a chance to get to know them."

"I'm sorry, Dad, it wouldn't work. Let's leave it, shall we?"

He was twenty-one when he married and moved to another suburb. His father hated the girl and her family and was pleased, two years later, when his son told him they were separating. Although he did not say "I told you so," nor did he say he was sorry. Fortunately, there were no children.

"Now you can look around for a nice girl of your own sort," he said, "then perhaps I'll see more of you."

"You could have seen a lot more of us if you'd wanted to." A note of bitterness had crept into the son's voice. "Anyway, I won't be around to see anyone."

"What do you mean?" his father asked sharply.

The son screwed his face up against the bright sky, then looked at the ground. "I'm going to do a bit of travelling, Dad. I need to be sure that I really belong here before I try settling down again."

"Course you belong. Australia's your future."

"Maybe, but as I said I need to be sure." He glanced at his father. "Sorry, Dad, but I don't want to end up like you, living life through memories and regrets." Then he was gone.

The man had his work to occupy him. He'd never been one to question his own actions - too much like all this psychoanalysis stuff and he wouldn't have a bar of that - but in his loneliness he couldn't help thinking about what his son had said. It was true, he'd clung to the past, when all the time the most important memories should have been those he was making with his son.

"Waste of precious time," he muttered to himself, and for the first time he felt a sense of gratitude for the scent of warm eucalyptus leaves, the cascading scarlet bottlebrush, the carolling of magpies, everything that his new country offered.

Not long afterwards, his son phoned to tell him father he was sick of travelling and that he was returning to Australia. The man surprised them both with an apology: "Sorry, son. Bloody idiot I've been all these years."

"You're right, Dad, and you're going to have to work hard to make up for it," the young man laughed. "You can start by finding those old prawning nets!"

And the man felt humbled, not only by this second chance to share time with his son and to create fresh memories but by his new understanding. Home, he sensed now, had nothing to do with your beginnings – it was the place that welcomed you and waited, for however long it took, for you to find where you belonged.

Marilyn Rainier

The Scent of Bluebells

I froze. My father's angry voice. I heard him leaving his study as he shouted for my mother. I glanced outside. A lovely day, bright and sunny. I was in luck.

Ignoring the churning in my stomach, I got up from the sofa where I had been sitting, placed my book quietly on the coffee table and made for the front door. What had caused his rage this time I didn't know and I certainly didn't want to stay to find out. I needed to disappear as quickly as I could, make myself scarce until, hopefully, the mood had passed. My mother would know where I was and why I had left.

We lived on a farm in the heart of the Kentish countryside in England; three hundred acres of fields and farmhouse, plus outbuildings – and one hundred acres of woodland. Leaving the house behind, I ran down the front path to the farmyard, past the stables and the old barn that separated the yard from the fields. There was rarely any traffic and I had no time to check now as I crossed the narrow road that separated the yard from the fields. Safely across, my eyes scanned the woods on the other side of the field in front of me. Tall trees – beeches, chestnuts, oaks and ash. They grew close together, as if to keep out strangers, but I knew the way in. I stumbled in my haste to climb over the ruts in the ploughed field. Another two minutes and I would be there I reassured myself. A footpath wound through the undergrowth. Leaving the field behind me, I followed the path and entered the darkness.

Narrowing my eyes as I tried to focus, the light through the trees showed me what I was looking for.

Bluebells! Not hundreds but thousands of them! During the spring and early summer, they grew in every available patch under the trees. I never ceased to wonder at it as I moved away from the earthiness of the ploughed field into the blue heaven that was my summer woods.

Kneeling down now, I touched the bells gently. The effect was immediate. No anger, no fear, simply peace. Bluebells do not survive in water, so I never remember a beautiful vase full of bluebells; only an ocean of them at my feet. They have bright, spiky leaves but this emerald green is almost totally hidden by what my mother once described to me as a carpet of Persian blue. The fun of it was to search for the rare bluebells – the white ones which dotted the carpet. I would count them until I ran out of numbers, then move on to search for yellow primroses and purple violets sheltering under bushes. These I often picked for my mother. But not now, I told myself. Not now.

Primroses and violets were sweet-smelling but the bluebell had a slightly acrid smell. Primroses and violets had tiny, frail stems and picked neatly, but bluebells had thick, juicy stems and produced a sticky, unpleasant sap. I understood that bluebells didn't want to die in vases and jam jars, so I knew the sap was intended to discourage the would-be picker and never broke that rule.

Walking carefully along the path, so I wouldn't tread on them, I wondered if bluebells knew about roses and envied them their thorns. I knew I wished I had thorns. No-one would touch us then. No-one would shout in that threatening way. I would defend my mother, scratch my father's face until it bled. And one day, when I was grown up, I would get a job, make some money, and we would leave. That would be the final thorn. Forgetting to tread carefully, I kicked at clods of earth along the path. Soon it would be dark and I would be in trouble if I stayed out late but a plan was forming in my mind. I knew now where I was headed and I began to run.

Moments later, I recognised the spot and came to a sudden stop. There it was. I looked around me carefully. No-one in sight. Crawling under the bushes, I touched the metal cage. Yes, a rabbit was pinned inside, held down across its hind legs by a metal bar.

The farm workers, on my father's orders, set these traps around the woods.

"Damned rabbits eating the crops!" my father would say. "We need a dose of myxomatosis. Finish them off."

My mother stayed silent. Not only was she afraid but there was no point in arguing. It was 1949. Even I knew that the only valid opinion was his.

I opened the cage door and lifted the bar away from the pinned legs. The rabbit moved. I exhaled. Thankfully, it was still alive.

Reaching inside the cage, I gripped the small, furry bundle, pulling it carefully away from the steel spring that had hinged the metal strut. Soon I had it outside the cage. I held it close to me, aware of its soft fur, its warmth, and its rapid breathing.

"There you are, Bunny," I said, as I placed it gently on the ground facing the track through the undergrowth. "Can you still hop?"

The rabbit moved forward, dragging its right hind leg. It stopped, obviously in pain, but I didn't touch it. I knew its only hope was to get to its burrow in order to heal before its scent reached a fox or some other hungry creature.

"Shoo, Bunny!" I said urgently, flapping my hands in its direction. "Go!"

It turned its face towards me for a split second, whether asking for help or to say thank you I wasn't sure. *How to tell it my powers were limited. It was on its own now.* I waved my hands again and this time it took a leap forward, still dragging a leg but now intent on escape. I watched as it disappeared in the undergrowth.

Relieved, I checked the cage again, careful to leave the door open. The trap was no longer set but that would mean nothing to the farm worker who checked it each morning. Any animal passing close by could have set it off by burrowing under the cage to reach the food placed inside rather than entering through the doorway.

No-one would guess a rabbit had been trapped or that I had played a part in its escape.

I crawled back under the bushes and scrambled to my feet, brushing off the earth clinging to my dress. I felt the sweet taste of victory as I retraced my steps. A nod of approval from the bluebells as I passed by reinforced my sense of wellbeing.

Here, in the peace of the woods, I had a sense of belonging no-one could take away from me. I felt sure my father's anger would have burnt out by now. Lucky Bunny.

Lucky me. I began to skip. A quick bunch of violets for my mother and I would be home in time for tea.

Marilyn Rainier

Gypsy Stories

I remember this particular day because my mother talked about when she was a girl and usually she would just brush questions away with a 'what do you want to know that for?' So this day I was sitting on the front step in charge of my brothers who were playing rounders with the kids from up the way when the gypsy lady came by. I recognised her because she came sometimes and always wanted to talk to Mum.

She asked if Mum was in and I said I would call her from the laundry. I liked her because she always called us lovelies. So she just stood there and waited with her bags and her hands full of heather while I went to find Mum.

I always liked the way my mother had different faces and how quickly she could change them. When I told her it was the gypsy lady, her tired look changed to what I called - stop everything and let's be happy look. She hurried up the corridor wiping her hands, and put her arms around the gypsy lady.

"Hallo, Bess."

"Brought some heather, Winifred – from Somma."

"Angel. Let us smell. Mmm - nothing like it. Come on in and sit. We'll have a nice pot."

"Had one at Number 11. Would not let me go."

"Stewed?"

"Well …"

"Got some one-cup cake. Come on. Don't let those boys out of your sight, Fanny."

And so I was back at the front step. Back to reading our Beano and watching, between pages, the boys: loud as ever, cheating whenever they could. I could hear Mum and the gypsy lady talking and laughing and thought it was nice to hear Mum called Winifred and realising that mothers actually had names other than just Mum. And Winifred, my mother, laughing: well it was like church bells.

And then I was thinking about the gypsy boy in Llanilar and that I had not thought of Wales for a while and that it would be nice not to have to watch the boys and just listen to the men singing in the Chapel. I always felt sad that Llanilar was somewhere I would probably never see again and thought I had never told Mum about the gypsy boy although we did talk about the Evans' when we had a letter.

And then suddenly it seemed, because I was dreaming of the Evans', the gypsy lady Bess was going with a bag I knew would have our old stuff in it. Mum saying to give her wishes to "you know who," and them both laughing and the lady saying – see you in Somma Winifred and Mum looking sad and her saying – one day. And then the gypsy Bess lady, said, looking at me, "She is a traveller, Winifred. She will leave us all behind." And my mother saying, "I know. She is always somewhere else, even sitting there."

We waved goodbye and watched Bess wandering over to the corner shop and then turning into the Crescent. Mum sat down on the step beside me, just sat there, not moving to go back to the washing. There was a lovely quiet and I looked at her and could see she was remembering, so I let her be. Then came that sighing which meant better get back, but before she could move, I said,

"I sat by a gypsy boy at school, Mum, not this school, but with Mr. Evans."

"You did? You never told me. What was his name?"

"Peter, well it really was Pierre. He was French. He had crossed the Channel in a boat to get away from the war."

So I told Mum how Pierre and Stephanie's parents had asked

Mr. Evans to have them in school and Pierre sat beside me, so I could help with his English. I told her that when I first saw him, all the girls ran away screaming.

"What on earth for?"

"They just kept screaming. A gypsy! A gypsy! They were stupid girls, Mum."

"Sounds like it. So what happened?"

So then I told Mum about when I was sitting on the bench outside the corner shop waiting for Mr. Evans and reading *Five on a Treasure Island.* Some of the girls were sitting on the grass playing bones. They had got a sherbet lick and were passing it around. I knew I wouldn't get a lick because they were annoyed I did not join in the game. They had ganged up to try to beat me.

I knew they would go as soon as the lick was finished and I hoped it would be soon. But they went much sooner because Betsy Morrison looked up and screamed, pointing down the road.

"It's the Gypsy boy! The Gypsy boy!"

They were up, running over the common, and into Betsy's back garden before I could even make out the boy coming along the road. The sun was in my eyes so I could not see him until he was almost at the door of the shop.

I can still see him. He was the most beautiful boy I had ever seen. I mean really lovely. I am not saying that our boys were not lovely, but they were just boys, ordinary boys, but this boy was just like I thought Tom would be in *The Water Babies*: something special.

He stopped just beside me, smiled and held out his hand. In it was a thruppenny bit. He seemed so happy. "You going to buy some sweets?" He nodded. So I went into the shop with him to see what he would buy.

Mr. Thomas said, "Hallo young Fanny. Waiting for the Headmaster then? Hallo young man. You'll be wanting some of our homemades. What'll be?"

The gypsy boy just looked at the sweet jars and then Mr. Thomas began speaking to him in Welsh, well it sounded Welsh, but was different and the gypsy boy replied in the same way. "Ah!" said Mr. Thomas and started filling a paper bag with a mixture from each of the jars. "You better get some broken biscuits Fanny. Here's a bag. You'll be going to chapel I think with him. Mrs. E. is in Aber today, is she not?"

I said yes Mrs Evans was in Aber shopping and watched him fill the bag with a rainbow mixture for the gypsy boy. When he was done he gave the gypsy boy the bag and then spoke to him while he made another rainbow bag and handed this to him as well. I understood him when he said it was for his sister. Then the gypsy boy gave Mr. Thomas the thruppenny bit and said, "Diolch Mister." I told him, "Hwyl fawr." He just smiled and went away with his bags of sweets.

"They have had a bad time Fanny. Crossed The Channel in a row boat. They are staying up behind Davydd's place and helping him out." He said they found things difficult because everyone wanted them to move on and away but that they were good people.

And then I told Mum we just went to Chapel with milk and broken biscuits, but I was thinking about the boy and coming across the Channel in a boat. "Did you teach him much English?" I told her yes, but it was just a few weeks before we all had to come back because the war was over. "I know you miss Wales lovely, but we have to try to get back to being a family again. Daddy will be home soon and we will all be together."

So then we just sat going back to being quiet again with Mum having that remembering look. We sat looking at the boys but I know we were somewhere else. Then Mum said, "You know Bess and your Aunt Daisy are sisters. Daisy and me – well we grew up together, but we are not what they would call – real sisters. But then you see, real sisters are made in heaven and Bess, Daisy and your Mum are real sisters."

And so Mum told me about how Bess and Daisy came to be in different families when they were growing up. How their parents were called Annie and Billy, but Billy was from a different gypsy group to Annie's. When she was having Bess, Annie told her family that she was going to live with Billy, away from her group and his. Everyone was against this, especially her mother who was a leader. Annie was very young and had to leave Bess and go with Billy. It was just done. I asked Mum if she would ever leave one of us like that. She just laughed and said not in a million but it was the way things were then.

When Annie was having my Aunt Daisy, Billy was killed working in the circus. My grandmother met Annie when they were working in a factory. Annie moved in with Nanny Boo because she was on her own. Then Daisy was born but Annie died soon after. So Nanny Boo brought up Aunt Daisy as her own with Mum and Uncle Barney. So that's how they are now sisters.

I told Mum I thought that was sad and she said sometimes things just happened. "Like the war," I said. "No, the things that happen to families just happen sometimes. It can't be helped. War is not the same because war should not happen, never." Mum had that face which said that she was cross, so I said no more.

She was quiet and then quietly said that she was sorry she was cross, "But when men have to go and fight and families are left to be bombed and people like Pierre and his family have to get in a boat and try to find a place where they will be not be taken and put into camps, there is something wrong with the world. We should always welcome travellers."

And then I asked her why gypsy Aunt Bess called me a traveller. Mum gave me one of her *I know what you are thinking my girl* looks, and said. "Well, there are travellers like Bess who seem to have to keep moving from hill to valley taking their homes with them to be content. Then there are other travellers, like you, who can travel into different worlds, into your books, away from where you are, just sitting in your chair or on the step. That is what Bess meant. She just has to look at you to know it. I know it because I am your Mum."

We sat looking at the boys, all quiet, me thinking about war and Peter; Llanilar and if I would see it again; travelling and gypsies, and then Mum turned to me. "Fanny: I think our boys are cheating."

Frances Richardson

John Harvard's Statue

The handsome face, immediately admired, expectant, learnéd: looking forward. The clothes plain, what a good Christian man, for this is what he was, would wear.

His book, open on the knee, has thick curled pages typical, one would think, of pages printed four centuries ago. The other books, beneath his chair, signify his library: Harvard's first library.

His shoes with tassels are from children's books, where everyone wore, like the prince in Cinderella, medieval clothes.

But the toe of his left shoe stands out. It is golden - not from design of Daniel Chester French, the sculptor – but from the touch of hands, mainly tourists - who then freeze the moment to stand beneath him.

They look up at the face, which was never his for we have no picture of this man, and touch the toe of his left foot. Perhaps this takes a little of what he represents into their lives.

This statue is not of John Harvard, nor did he found the college, but loved the idea. The statue has a wonderful history of those who, two centuries after he died, wished to remember someone who was a part of Harvard's history. To them, the history of learning in Massachusetts mattered.

John Harvard, a graduate of Cambridge and a religious exile from England, was the first benefactor of the college. He died aged 30 in 1638: he had spent only thirteen months in the new world.

Frances Richardson

Written 2014 when studying a unit at Harvard.

Travelling South – Western Australia

From a home, flat to the dry land
arid, tenuous
surrounded by marri, wandoo
blinding quartz sand, grass trees and cycads
I head south for respite

Avoiding the city on new highways
relaxation begins when finally
leaving these roads to recovery
I pass fields, yes fields. English fields
lush with grass, fat sheep, and picturesque cattle

Poplars line avenues
horses graze under Lebanon cedars
Veldt daisies explode from gardens

and then …
            the slow turn of a rusty windmill

Harvey welcomes with a young boy's Pears' complexion
His smile is peach rosy,
a product of healthy milk
from an iconic dairy
ever flowing from a Hardy Somerset

I wander a cottage garden
my feet brush lavender and nasturtiums
my hair touches jasmine, wisteria, climbing roses
I cross Wilton House soft lawns to a gentle fountain sound
watch plump mallards cruise the Blackwood River

I have been taken to a northern hemisphere
terrain altered to produce pictorial villages
It is a Cotswold meander through a garden county

and then …
the bright flash of the Splendid Wren

Tempted by an art sign
I prise my way through pathways
of Victorian furniture
brown, musty, pushed together -
over-priced repros for antique buyers
beneath bygone-age prints from London

Still in another time, another country
I eat apple pie
drink English breakfast tea

and then …
    the slow slide of a black lizard through cape weed
    the demanding stance of a young magpie

I turn into a Welsh valley
bathed in a spring sunset
change into a rarely used low gear
to climb a hill a camber
the Camry has rarely scaled

Halfway I slow to see the valley lake
small water catchments below catch blue light
downs slope to neat espaliered pear trees
and what may be peaches, plums, and Jonathon apples
just greening

A final curve, more poplars, an oak tree
an English voice and welcome
the scent of again lavender, nasturtiums and larkspur

and then ...
    the chalet amid the red gums

The trees are tall, charred, remote
much younger than my marri
late sun sparkles through their high crowns
the gravel smell is damp

My hand trails the rust on the barbie,
the other grey rough bark
I follow the familiar slow upward
settling flight of a kookaburra

It looks down
and then …
            the swift plunge to the prey below

Frances Richardson

June 1944

The memories of soft sandy beaches, boats in the harbour, flowers, sunsets over the water, family dinners, warmth of affection and the call of home were ever present. It was his place, Weymouth in England.

Leaving home to do his bit to help during World War II, he enlisted at 17, registered his occupation as schoolboy, as did his friend and classmate. Both were assigned to a ship in the Royal Navy.

He wasn't tall, just over five foot four and his appearance inconspicuous with his fair hair and grey eyes he was just another young face among many in the crowd leaving for overseas service.

The ship was a minesweeper and the men on board became a replacement family. Fear, hard work, necessity, and duty bound them together until one day it didn't.

They were separated and he fell into the hands of the enemy as a prisoner of war. He was taken to a place in Malaya where he would meet other prisoners who were destined to become a family.

Surrounded by jungle, smothered by heat and humidity, and tortured by strangers he survived there for two years until he was identified as suitable to travel to work on the railway of death.

He boarded another ship. Crammed into tiny spaces in the ship's hold beneath deck they were desperate for air, water, and food. Huddled together, squashed on top of each other, it was impossible for any air to reach them. The smell of human stench was unbearable.

A few hours later a sound crashed into their world of misery, blasting their ears, and racking their bodies. A torpedo hit the ship and split it in two halves. He was in the half that went straight to the bottom of the ocean.

Finally, aged 31 years, he had a place where he could rest in peace.

Back home his family in Weymouth gazed upon the Portsmouth Naval Memorial and remembered him. In their hearts he had never left. He was there amidst the boats in the harbour, the flowers, the soft sandy beaches and the watery sunset.

Stephanie Slanzi

A Place to Call Home.

"There is snow on the Great Western Tiers". A phrase in a letter from Tasmania brought a surge of memories, memories of our family home, when my siblings and I were young more than seventy years ago.

In 1946 our father re-joined the family having reached the retiring age for those serving with the Indian Medical Service. With India about to become independent, it was time to move on. We spent the rest of that year in Geelong where, with our mother, we had been living through the war years. In January of 1947, leaving the dry dusty heat of Geelong, we moved to Westbury in Tasmania. Our father had bought a run-down general practice there. He was intending to work for himself instead of a government body. This was one of the reasons we had not returned to the UK once the war was over. He was also a keen fisherman and looked forward to fishing on the Great Lake.

Westbury is a small country town about 20 miles (28 kms) west of Launceston, situated on the Bass Highway. This was the main road from Launceston to Wynyard in the west. Highway was perhaps a misnomer as in those days it was just a normal two-lane sealed road connecting the towns and villages in northern part of Tasmania. A proper highway now by-passes many of these places along the route.

When we moved in that January of '47, we three girls were still enrolled at boarding schools or colleges on the mainland. Rather than change to Tasmanian schools, our parents decided we would stay on in our places of learning. This was disappointing. The distance and expense of travel being too great meant we could no longer go home for the half term exeats or boarders' weekends. We could only travel home for the proper term holidays. We missed the changing seasons in Westbury. After the summer holidays we were next home for the cold wet May holidays. Then by the time we were there again in September, spring was nearly over, so we missed the trees in bloom. I'd had hopes of becoming a weekly boarder at a Launceston school, but that was not to be.

Farmland surrounded Westbury. With the cooler climate the early settlers had tried to recreate a part of the England they remembered by planting deciduous trees and setting hawthorn hedges between the paddocks. These hedges had become overgrown forming thin barriers of trees as the property owners no longer kept them in shape.

There to the South, in the background were the Western Tiers with their majestic peaks outlined against the sky. It was so different from Geelong where we had been living for six years surrounded by other houses with traffic and trams on the streets. There was so much more space here in Westbury and little traffic due to petrol rationing.

Our property had a large orchard behind the house and there were empty blocks on either side. Our father leased one of these and on that we kept a jersey cow – Polly. When home for the school holidays we would take over the milking, separating and butter-making. Over the road in front was the Village Green. There was no duck pond, but the Meander River flowed on the far side. In the riverbanks, sheltered by weeping willow trees, platypus lived. Occasionally, in the evening if the hopeful viewers remained quiet they might see one.

In front of the Tiers was a low range of hills, and behind these the section of the Tiers showed two of the many peaks – Drysdale Bluff and Quamby Bluff. Quamby Bluff was the closest and more easily visible from our house on the western side of the township and it remained a landmark and symbol of home. Its rugged shape silhouetted against the sky. When we had first arrived, at the turning to our road we saw a road sign 'Snow Road Closed'. This was January! Our father said the council had probably forgotten to take the sign down. Even so we could see a small patch of snow high up on Quamby Bluff in a sheltered spot where the sun had not reached.

Our parents were keen gardeners. After years of living in rented houses or in residences supplied by the place of work, they at last had a home of their own. Mother soon had the front garden under control. She was keen on irises but had lots of other flowers as well. Our father looked after the orchard, grew vegetables and berry fruits. In the summer there was always a plentiful supply of raspberries. The apricots often ripened just before Christmas. Mother would be busy making jam on Christmas Eve. Many years later I found myself doing the same thing as our own small orchard here on the farm would produce apricots at that time. In his youth in Ayrshire, Father had helped on the local farms during holidays from school and university. Now at last, having his own property, he could put his skills to use. He showed us how to scythe the long grass in the orchard and how make it into stooks with the pitchfork. We also scythed the thistles and sorrel in the rented paddock. Later he put in a small oat crop and showed us how to tie the oats up before stooking them. No doubt useful skills, but I have never had to use them since. It was hard to leave at the end of the holidays.

I always hoped I would be able to sit on the right-hand side of the plane when I was coming home so I. could look out for the first glimpse of Quamby Bluff as it stood serenely in its place. Then later, having landed and continuing the journey by bus, or by car if I were lucky, I would keep a look out, watching the range of hills and the two bluffs behind it line up in the right configuration. When they were in the right place, I knew I would be home at last. Though we were only about the same distance from Launceston as our farm here was from Mt Barker (about 28 kilometres) the journey seemed to take longer. This was probably because we passed through more villages on the way and, due to closer settlement, there would have been more traffic, even in those days.

The places from Launceston were Carrick, Hadspen with the Entally Historic House, and the bridge over the Esk River. Then Hagley where the Farm School was situated, and the spire of St Mary's Church stood out from the surrounding flat countryside. Nearly there, then at last Westbury. We would pass Fitzpatrick's Village Inn and some more shops and houses. Then on the left the Catholic Church – a big bluestone building (established in 1870) with the presbytery nearby. The church had a clock tower and in the quiet of the night one could hear it strike, marking the hours. An empty block of land on the corner was where the original school had been situated. Then round the corner and The Village Green was on the right-hand side and on the other, there was our house. Home at last – bliss.

Petrol rationing was in force and though, as a doctor, our father had extra petrol coupons, he would not use the car for such frivolous purposes as collecting us from the Western Junction Airport. We had to catch the airways bus into Launceston and wait for the bus back to Westbury. The bus catered for those working in Launceston so left Westbury soon after 8.00 am and did not return there till late afternoon. This often meant a long wait at the CWA rooms till it was time to heft our suitcases up to the bus depot. On reaching Westbury, the driver would turn the bus just before the Catholic Church and deposit the passengers outside the Meaghan's General Store. Our father would meet us there with the car if a patient had not called him for a home visit

Though expensive, we generally flew back and forth. This

would give us a little longer time at home. I found the quick change from home to school or vice versa stressful and was glad when occasionally the situation required me to travel by sea. The journey of course did take longer but it was much more enjoyable and gave one a clean break between home and school. Back then it was miniature sea voyage on the old M.V Taroona. The ship left Melbourne at about 4.00 pm and took some time heading down Port Philip Bay. It was sensible to go to the first sitting for dinner which was a proper meal in the dining room. The sea became rough once the ship had moved between the Heads (Points Lonsdale and Nepean) and then into and through the Rip to Bass Strait. It was always exciting to watch the leading lights as we went through and to see how they lined up when the ship turned to navigate through the heads.

I knew better than to book a berth on the lowest level C deck. It was cheaper, but B deck was quite low enough. I would stay on deck breathing in the fresh air for as long as I could and hoping I would make the journey without being seasick. Soon after breakfast the next morning, the ship would dock at Wynyard or Burnie. Then there was the train to catch. The Tasmanian gauge was the same as the WA one being the narrow 3' 6" railway track. It was a pretty journey with the steam train rattling along. The narrow track was quite close to the sea and in some places almost on the beach. It stopped at small towns along the way and eventually reached Westbury. Home once again.

Now it has all changed. There is a big ferry and it is no longer a miniature sea voyage, but just a means of getting across Bass Strait. The last time we took family was in the late 70's. Again, it has changed and now one can cross in daylight. The Bass Highway bypasses Westbury and cuts across the other side of Hadspen, so the Entally Homestead is no longer visible from the road. This is probably an improvement as, in the winter, if the Esk River flooded, vehicles would have to make a big detour.

Letters from my mother at that time of the year would often refer to the floods and the difficulty of getting to Launceston on the weekly trip. The new road by-passes the town on the southern side so the traffic in winter can avoid the flooded river.

A few years ago, my husband and I did a tour of Tasmania visiting places we had not been to before. We flew over and hired a car. I found myself looking out of the plane window and there was Quamby Bluff still standing majestically welcoming me back.

Alison P. Smith.

Graveyard

We have come to a place where the seabirds make their nests from strands of cold metal wires. They have no other choice, you see. Life here is all about surviving one day to hopefully work the next. Thin limbed, dark skinned, huge eyed, hungry children of twelve work alongside their elders, their small size enabling them to squeeze into places no adult can. They are proud to be able to contribute a few cents per hour to the family coffers. Welcome to the Chittagong ship-breaking yards of Bangladesh, where the once proud giants of the sea come to die.

Chittagong lies in southeastern Bangladesh on the edge of the Bay of Bengal. With a population of four million, Chittagong is the second largest city in the country. It is a major coastal seaport and the financial centre of southeastern Bangladesh. A few short miles north of the city more than eighty ship-breaking yards ply their ugly industry, filling an eight mile stretch of once pristine coastal beach.

Little is required for ship-breaking in Bangladesh today: a simple crane or derrick, a few blow-torches and if workers are lucky, a bulldozer. Cheap and exploitable human labour provides the main component. If a person is killed or maimed, well, that is no problem: there is a vast pool of humans waiting to take their place.

The workers come from the northern parts of Bengal, the poorest areas. Farmers desperate to feed their families leave their land for the ship-breaking yards. Here, uneducated and unqualified, with no knowledge of their rights, they work up to sixteen hours a day, seven days per week for an average wage of twenty-five cents an hour or four dollars a day. The top wage is forty-seven cents per hour—for the lucky ones.

When asked why they continue to migrate to the ship-breaking yards, the reply from the workers is simple. If a man goes to the yards then yes, perhaps he will die from an accident, but if he remains at home, then five people will die from starvation. It is impossible to make a living from his farm or in his local village so what choice does he have? A man who is any sort of a man must feed his family.

These men and their families get their strength and courage from their religion. The women visit the mosques daily to pray to Allah. In their prayers they thank Allah for giving their men and boys work, they thank Allah when these same men and boys survive a bad accident and they ask for courage to face each day. These people consider themselves blessed when a day passes without injury to family members.

Today, more than half the world's large ships come to Bangladesh to die an inglorious death. Ninety-five percent of a ship can be recycled making it one of greatest sources of revenue for a poverty stricken country with a population of 163 million. Bangladesh needs steel, having no iron ore of its own. Ship-breaking provides more than eighty percent of the country's steel needs.

The yards are ruled by fear. Often the city mayor will own a yard causing local government to look the other way and ignore the daily atrocities. There is no job training, no unions, no decontamination facilities or monitoring, no form of medical care or attention, no protective laws for the workers, no hygiene, no compensation for injury or death, no cremation payments for families of dead workers. It is much cheaper to throw the dead bodies into the sea. People vanish all the time, just disappearing from the official statistics. Protecting workers costs money. Human life does not. Government at all levels is prepared to turn the other cheek.

Life is cheap and brutal in the shipping graveyards where threat of job loss keeps most workers quiet. Access to the ships is via rope ladder. The men work with bare hands and feet and use no safety equipment at all. Every hour of the day they are exposed to gas explosions, falling steel plates, asbestos, heavy metals such as mercury, lead, cadmium, zinc and copper and toxic oil and fuels. Burning of various wastes exposes workers to Polycyclic Aromatic Hydrocarbons (PAHs), many of which are carcinogenic.

The workers live in makeshift huts constructed from remnants of their trade, such as asbestos. Both water and food are contaminated. Asbestos is found in many places on these ships, its resistance to heat, its strength and durability, making it a preferred material for making fire proof doors, engine casings, electrical cable sheeting, boiler casing packings, exhaust pipe packings, sandwich panels in corridors and mounting panels on electrical heaters, to name but a few of its uses.

Bilge water is a combination of fresh water, sea water, oil, sludge and chemicals which accumulate in the lowest part of the ship's hull, the bilge wells. It can contain cargo residue, inorganic salts, arsenic, copper, chromium, lead and mercury. Bilge water is pumped out directly into the ocean, adding to an already heavily contaminated coastal zone. Fish from these seaside waters is a major source of food for workers.

Once ship-breaking belonged mainly to the industrialised nations, primarily the United States, United Kingdom, Germany and Italy. But in the early 1980s, greedy ship owners found a much cheaper way: send their vessels to the yards of India, China, Pakistan, Bangladesh, the Philippines and Vietnam, where men desperate for work would slave for a pittance, where there were no health or safety standards and where people were expendable. Another factor came into play: governments of developed countries wished to rid themselves of the industry since it did not comply with the new environmental protection standards. Industrialists in countries such as Bangladesh were quick to embrace ship-breaking with its massive profits. No major investment was required and the people and the environment were ripe for exploitation in such a country.

Today, in the second decade of the twenty-first century, Southern Asia is the world centre of the ship-breaking and recycling industry. Eighty percent of large tankers and container ships are scrapped in Bangladesh, India and Pakistan. China and Turkey account for fifteen percent with only five percent of the world volume being scrapped outside these five countries.

Each new ship that is driven onto the beach means employment for the hungry, more money for the owners. The ships holds many tanks and chambers which contain oil, petroleum and poisonous gases. First, the level of danger has to be checked: a living animal is lowered down by rope to see if it can survive the poisonous gases. If the animal does not die, the first worker will be lowered down to 'check the danger level'. He has no instruments or equipment to help him in this so-called assessment.

If the first worker gives the all-clear, has not collapsed or died, the first group of workers will enter the ship to clean away the oil, petroleum and other flammable substances. Anything that can be burned off will be so. Explosions are a common occurrence. Next the cutters enter the ship to break it into huge pieces. Once the tide drops, dozens of workers tug these massive steel plates ashore where they are then cut into much smaller pieces. These pieces are then sent to the factories for recycling. The workers use blow torches and wear no gloves, goggles, shoes or hard hats. The smoke, fumes and heat add to the savagery of the working environment.

There is no family at the Chittagong yards that has not lost a brother, cousin, son, father, friend or fellow worker to fatal accident. Body bags are a common sight. Then there are the non fatal incidents: one serious accident per day in each yard is the norm. These result in severed limbs, crushed toes and feet, spinal injuries, blindness, ripped away fingers and hands and severe burns, and this is just the beginning. Then there are the illnesses which take longer to appear: exposure to toxic chemicals can harm the nervous system, cause mental retardation, affect neurological and physical development in children, impair vision and hearing, damage muscle coordination, cause cancer, harm the lungs and heart and impair the immune system. We must not forget mesothelioma, a rare and very aggressive form of cancer which develops in the lining of the lungs, abdomen or heart, nor asbestosis, a lung disease resulting from the inhalation of asbestos particles, and so the list goes on and on and on…

Official statistics differ greatly from those obtained by the investigative journalists brave enough to venture into the yards of Chittagong but unofficially, it is estimated that the industry employs up to 200,000 workers. If a worker from the yards talks to a journalist, he will lose his job. There have been instances where workers have been prepared to help journalists access the protected yards: these helpful workers usually mysteriously vanish. Outsiders are not wanted behind the high, razor wire topped fences and any show of interest or curiosity, let alone the appearance of a camera, will be warned off at gun point.

Young Power in Social Action (YPSA), a non-government organisation, has begun work to address the basic needs and rights of workers in the ship-breaking yards. They are the first organisation to attempt to tackle the problem and the first successful changes are coming through the women.

YPSA encourages women to meet to discuss the main problems of daily living and helps them to implement suggested changes. Some yard workers now have access to clean water for drinking, cooking and hygiene and clean, free community bathrooms, thanks to their women. Before this, hundreds of yard families had to share a filthy community bathroom and pay local government a daily fee for the privilege. The only other option was the contaminated sea for bathing and personal bodily functions.

The United Nations agency, the International Labour Organisation (ILO) has also begun to take notice, although it has been remarkably slow to do so. It seems to be quite efficient at writing charters to document preferred conditions for the workers of the ship-breaking yards but actually putting such things into practise appears to be much more difficult.

These once mighty queens of the ocean are born with such ceremony, a tradition dating back to before the birth of Christ. Christened with a bottle of champagne at the hands of a lovely lady, they majestically slide into the sea to the applause of an adoring audience. It is both a blessing and a public celebration: the crowds wave and cheer, the cameras click and roll and the occasion is committed to print. Humans are humble before these glamorous mammoths of the sea.

But these modern giants have an average lifespan of twenty-six years. Each year around thirteen hundred ships die on the beaches of some of the poorest countries in the world. It is an inglorious death: they are driven hard onto the shore, deliberately beached, dumped on poisoned sands amidst the partially stripped carcasses of their sister ships. There they end their days, to be broken on the beaches of Chittagong and her like.

There is a proverb from the ship-breaking yards of Alang in India: *Every day one ship, every day one dead.* There is little need to say more.

Ingrid M. Smith

References:
Bob Simon *60 Minutes*
National Geographic
RTD Documentary Channel
Mark Knopfler *So Far From the Clyde*

The Blessing

1972

The Blessing ceremony would be held at the Cameron farm. The whole district buzzed in anticipation.

The women brushed and sponged the best suits of their menfolk before looking to the needs of their children and finally, themselves. Best frocks were checked over; fresh collars and cuffs were stitched in place. Leather shoes were treed, polished and treed again before the final shine was applied. Children's frocks were made over so that only mothers would recognise the original garment.

The Cameron farm was one of the loveliest in the district; it was also one of the most profitable. The homestead lay snugly encircled by a large orchard. The pedigree Jersey herd lived a contented life on the gentle green slopes west of the river. The market garden supplied the general stores for many miles around. But the beating heart, the real lifeblood of the Cameron farm, was the sawmill.

Both farm and sawmill dated back to the 1860s when two Cameron brothers had been among the earliest settlers granted land in our district. Flourishing ironbark, mahogany, blackbutt and the much valued red cedar inspired the creation of the sawmill on the eastern bank of the small, but vigorous river that bisected the newly acquired land. For more than a century the Camerons had held farm and sawmill.

Blessing Sunday began like every Sunday; church at eight sharp followed by Sunday School. As the church slowly emptied, packed vehicles began making their way out to the Cameron farm. As soon as Rector Tate had shaken the final hand in the church porch, he collected his shabby leather liturgical bag and clambered into his battered Mini Cooper. His car was the last to leave the little old wooden church that morning.

The Cameron women had been preparing for weeks. Providing both lunch and afternoon tea for well over one hundred people takes some doing. Long trestle tables borrowed from the church hall were set up in the orchard, then covered with spotless white cloths. Mouth-watering chicken and mushroom casserole in vast tureens was backed by numerous salads, huge platters of cold ham and beef and home-baked breads. Mammoth dishes of apple pie followed, accompanied by plump glass jugs of pedigree Jersey herd cream.

Cathy Cameron was a close friend of mine. Extremely pretty with fair curls, lovely blue eyes and a softly rounded figure, she was feminine and gentle, the complete antithesis of me. Her grandparents currently lived at the farm, managing both it and the sawmill; they were the mainstay and backbone of the Cameron family.

Even more people had arrived by three in the afternoon, the hour of the Blessing. We children were chivied out of the old orchard, a youngster's paradise. Divided from the proper orchard by a thick hedge, neat lines of lichen-covered fruit trees lived out their final years here. Pear, apricot, apple, cherry and best of all, tangy citrus trees, created a magic kingdom for all children. We had been playing what started out as hide-and-go-seek but somehow turned into an armed battle, boys against girls, the fruit trees being our well armed fortresses. A brisk brush down; a wipe from a clean handkerchief withdrawn from a neat maternal handbag; a quick cuff from the odd impatient hand and we were all present and correct.

Grandfather Cameron led Rector Tate down the gentle slope

to the river, where the newly installed sawmill plant awaited. When we were all gathered at the riverbank, the Cameron men and their employees were asked to stand aside, making a semi-circle around the waiting machinery. The whole scene had that real Sunday feel about it; the women in their pretty dresses; the older women in broad brimmed hats; the men dignified in their Sunday suits; the children all beautifully turned out. I stood close to Cathy, who looked so sweet and pretty in her smocked dress of mauve cotton with a butterfly sash tied at the back. I was so proud of my smart Sunday shoes; they were ornamented with white leather daisies.

I looked at Rector Tate, the hem of his black, ankle length cassock lightly flapping in the gentle afternoon breeze. Medium height, middle-aged, stout and opinionated, he was the heart and soul of our small bush community. Every Tuesday his battered car chugged its way around the district, moving from farm to house, always going where he was needed most. It mattered not of what religion you were, Rector Tate embraced all. He was so much a part of our lives that perhaps we all took him for granted. I was about fifteen when he was found dead in his small dwelling one morning, and I know that our tight little community was never the same again. The next incumbent of the parish, who came from a big city, just never understood how a bush society operated.

As well as the three churches under his care, Rector Tate had started up local branches of the Church of England Boys Society (CEBS) and the Girls Friendly Society (GFS); there was also Friday night Youth Group. The latter, aimed at keeping young people out of trouble, was for high school students, and great fun. Rector Tate roped in two of our high school teachers to help him with the running, and one never knew what was in store on Friday nights, between seven and nine. The Sunday school thrived under his guidance. Rector Tate was backed by a small but vigorously enthusiastic committee but his was the guiding light.

Rector Tate was nearly always surrounded by a group of youngsters; they followed his rotund form everywhere. Today, I am sure, something mean, nasty and suggestive would be made of this, but not in those halcyon days. Quite simply, the man loved children and they loved him. Minutes earlier I had watched a group of boys vie for the honour of helping Rector Tate prepare for the Blessing. As I watched this remarkable man, he raised a hand for silence, and began to speak:

'We are gathered here today, both as a family and a community, to ask for your Blessing, Lord. Jesus showed us the dignity of work. He was known as the carpenter's son and He willingly worked with the tools of his trade. Through the labour of our hands, we bring God's blessing upon ourselves and others. Like Jesus, the men who work here work with wood, and labour with their hands. Let us pray for all who will work with this sawmill and for those who will share the fruit of their labours.'

'We ask this through Christ our Lord, Amen.'

He asked our Lord to protect all the men who worked with the new equipment and to keep them safe and free from accident. Using his beloved aspergillum, Rector Tate generously sprinkled the flanks of the new machinery plant.

The ceremony drew to its close. Grandfather Cameron's face shone with pleasure as he shook hands with Rector Tate. Silently the Cameron women slipped away, back to the homestead; the menfolk would be soon wanting their afternoon tea. Grandmother Cameron was noted throughout the district for her scones.

The men were reluctant to leave the mechanical wonders on the riverbank. No machine could be put to work on a Sunday but Cathy's dad was making descriptive movements with his hands, waving them around, this way and that. The men around him nodded, asked questions. Someone pointed at part of the new sawmill plant and Cathy's dad nodded vigorously, with more hand and arm movements.

I saw old Mr Evans, seated in the shade, his wife protectively at his side. He had survived the atrocities of Changi. Mr Richards, manager of the local cheese factory, stood next to him, keeping an unobtrusive eye open in case help was needed. These people, my people, always looked out for their own.

I glanced at my classmate, Sharon, who had two older cousins fighting in Vietnam. I could see my beloved teacher, Mrs Carr, with her family. Her French ancestry showed in the simple elegance of her costume. Under a stand of eucalypts stood the very thin, upright figure of Miss Clarkson, famed for purchasing a purebred Arabian stallion for three thousand dollars. The district didn't stop talking for many weeks.

My mother had slipped away with the Cameron women; my father was talking to the manager of the Estate Farms.

These were the people of my childhood and this was my world.

Ingrid M. Smith

From the City to the Bush

A blind date initiated my move from the city to the little rural district of Bow Bridge just west of Denmark on the south coast. I was born in 1933 in a little cottage type hospital in Inglewood in the metropolitan area and lived there until I married. The city was the only life I knew – country living was a total mystery to me at that time.

My workmate was asked to find a girl to make up a foursome with her cousin and his friend who were coming to Perth to see a show. I agreed to be that girl. We all had a very enjoyable night out although I did report to my mother later that my date was "very nice but a bit old!" He was twenty-four and I was just eighteen!

Our friendship developed and Bruce visited me regularly. I spent my holidays with him at his parents' home in Bow Bridge where Bruce and his father ran a sawmill primarily to cut fruit cases. On these visits, I learned a little of rural living and in between, we wrote long letters.

Love blossomed and we were eventually engaged but my mother insisted we wait until I was twenty-one before we married.

Our wedding in November 1954 was memorable and after a short honeymoon, we travelled to Bow Bridge to take up residence in a new timber cottage on Bruce's block of land. Population at Bow Bridge at that time was fairly scarce.

As a new bride from the city, I learned to deal with 'sides' of meat from a local farmer, rather than the neat little packages I had seen my mother buy from the butcher. Our milk came from a neighbour who milked a few cows and who delighted in telling me (with a definite twinkle in his eye) that "she's a good cow, that Molly!"

Our three daughters were born here, and I remember being very excited when a Bow Bridge family opened a little store and I could take my youngsters for a walk to pick up some bread!

When the youngest of our three daughters was just one year old, we moved to a farm which we had purchased in the Hazelvale district. Bruce's great love was farming and the sawmill was eventually sold.

We built a milking shed on the Hazelvale property and joined the dairy farmers of the district. We named the property *Carinya*, meaning happy home, and ran some beef cattle as well. Our son was born several years after we made the move to this farm.

As a city girl, dairying and farm life in general was a real challenge to me and I had a number of (in hindsight!) rather amusing experiences. I even wrote a book documenting the adventures of a city girl 'thrown in at the deep end'.

Finally, after some twenty years, we decided the time had come to relinquish the demanding dairying routine. We sold the farm in Hazelvale and retired to our land in Bow Bridge where we built a new brick home. Here, we ran beef cattle and started to explore Australia in our caravan and enjoy some overseas travel.

Parkinsons and Alzheimers disease eventually led to the necessity for Bruce to move into an aged care facility in Albany and I made the move there to be near him and assist with his care as much as possible.

He died in 2002 and I have continued to live in Albany but still own the Bow Bridge block and house and I spend time there regularly. What keeps me coming back? The fact that I had been in the area for forty-eight years and became very involved in district life: my son lives there and looks after my property: and the bonus is the proximity of Peaceful Bay - an idyllic coastal area. It is where my heart is – definitely my sense of place.

Molly Smith

The New House

A story for children and the young at heart

Foreword …

On a beautiful sunny day some years ago, I noticed a pair of Willie Wagtails being particularly active around a little brick shed near our house on my Bow Bridge property. They were flying busily in and out of the shed.

I didn't take a great deal of notice until sometime later when I watched a little family of wagtails doing the same. On investigation, I finally saw a perfect little nest built on top of the fluorescent light in the shed! With some fifteen or more beautiful bushy native trees in the garden, they had chosen this strange position.

I decided it was worthy of a story …

Willie Wagtail sat on a leafy branch of a beautiful grevillea bush and gave a long, worried sigh.

"Hey, careful. You nearly blew me off this branch!" said Bobby Blue Wren, smoothing his ruffled feathers. "Whatever is the matter?"

"Well," said Willie Wagtail, "as you know, it's nesting time and my darling wife Winnie can't make up her mind which of these beautiful bushes will be just right for our nest."

"Oh," said Bobbie. "Is this your first nest?"

"Yes, it is," replied Willie, looking a little self-conscious. "It's time we started and there she is fluttering from bush to bush, bypassing some wonderful leafy, well-hidden spots. Whatever is the matter with this one I am sitting in for instance? There are some ideal places to set up house." He gave another deep sigh.

"Women are like that," said Bobbie knowledgeably, "and if you suggest somewhere you may be sure she won't like it. My advice is to tuck your head into your wing for a while, have a little nap, and wait till she tells you what she has found."

With those words of wisdom, the little wren flew off to look for titbits for lunch.

Willie decided to find Winnie first to see how her search was going before he had his nap. There she was … flying in and out of a beautiful hakea.

"How are you going, my sweet?" Willie asked rather nervously.

"Oh, Willie, I just can't decide. There are so many wonderful nesting spots. I wish I could make up my mind."

"So do I," Willie twittered to himself. However, he lovingly replied, "Well, my dear, I think I will just wait in that grevillea over there until you find the ideal situation, and then you can show me."

Willie flew back to the grevillea and promptly drifted off to sleep. He was awakened by excited bird calls from his little mate.

"Oh, Willie, I have found the BEST place for our first home. Come with me and I will show it to you."

She flew off and Willie was surprised to see her disappear into a little brick shed near the house which was part of the tree-lined garden they had found.

"Up there," she said as Willie flew in behind her.

"Up where?" he said with a puzzled look.

Impatiently, Winnie flew high and came to rest on a long, white structure (which was actually a fluorescent light) hanging from the ceiling. Willie couldn't believe his eyes.

"But there are no leaves or branches … nothing to hide our nest," he said.

"But, Willie, no one will ever think of looking up there for a nest," Winnie said. "It's perfect."

"Well, my sweet, if that's what you want, that's where we will build it," and Willie flew up and landed beside his excited little mate. Winnie wrapped her little wings around him and gave him a big hug.

Winnie Wagtail couldn't wait to begin building the nest. In fact, nothing would satisfy her but an immediate start. She and Willie flew back and forth selecting just the right material and very soon a neat, strong nest sat atop the fluorescent light. The two birds admired their handiwork with delight.

"Oh, Willie, it's beautiful!" Winnie said excitedly.

"You're right, my dear, it really is a grand little home," Willie responded.

"Now I can lay my eggs," Winnie said, and waggled her tail in anticipation.

Willie decided to collect some titbits for his wife. She was sure to be exhausted after all her efforts. He flew off and when he returned, Winnie was sitting on the nest, her little body puffed out to cover the eggs she had cleverly laid inside.

"My dear," said Willie, "you have been busy! You are such a clever little wife. I've brought you some food. I must look after you whilst you hatch out our family. How many eggs have you laid?"

"Well, Willie, I have put three tiny eggs in the nest. Now I will have to sit quietly until it is time for our baby birds to tap on the shells and come into the world. I'm so excited I can't wait until we have our family and can teach them to fly."

"Now, now my dear … don't be in a rush! Everything comes in good time. You just sit there quietly, and I will make sure you are never hungry."

"Willie, you are so good to me. You are going to be the perfect father. Now I am rather sleepy so I will have a nap. You know there will be times when I will have to come off this nest to drink some water and stretch my legs and wings, but I certainly won't be leaving these precious eggs for too long. They would soon get cold and goodness me, our babies must have warmth to grow."

Time went by and Willie was most attentive to his little wife as she sat patiently on the nest waiting for the eggs to hatch.

One perfect spring morning, he returned from his hunt for food to find Winnie fluttering up and down, round and round, her little tail twitching in anticipation.

"Willie, Willie," she called, "our babies are breaking out of their eggs, do come and see!"

Willie quickly flew to his wife's side and peered into the nest. Sure enough, three tiny beaks could be seen and soon the eggs were just a mash of broken shell as three very small, very frail willie wagtail babies floundered around in the nest.

Willie couldn't take his eyes off his new family and he gave his wife a big wing hug to let her know how happy he was.

The weeks passed and the couple was kept busy feeding their small brood. Finally, the the day came to teach them to fly.

At first, the babies tottered around the edge of the nest, but gradually their tiny legs grew stronger and they learnt how to use their wings.

In no time at all, they were zooming around the garden enjoying this newfound freedom in a world of blue skies and leafy green bushes … just the right setting for a family of willy wagtails with a sense of place.

Molly Smith

Retreat into the Green Paddock

Journal Entry by Roger
Acknowledging, accepting and working with adversity are already in my genes! All four grandparents experienced hardship during both World Wars and the Depression. Natural disasters were not new for my parents either. They battled through drought or floods while slowly establishing a wheat and sheep farm from virgin land. Many times the bottom fell out of one or two markets and half of the income evaporated when wheat, wool and livestock entered the market. They could never win and their belts were continually tightened. While my mum and dad worked the land, they often took second jobs elsewhere to earn cash to buy the bare essentials. These memories of my childhood have always been tucked away in my mind. They've been of value throughout my life to date. More to Come Soon ~ Roger :))

Roger's birthday was in December so he'd always been the youngest class member during his schooling years. He scraped through his education on the bare minimum standards. At the end of every year, he was promoted and pushed up to the next year level. At the age of fifteen, Roger and his family breathed a sigh of relief. At long last it was legal for him to leave school. His parents had automatically thought he would stay home to help around the farm. But Roger was not having any of that.

With stars in his eyes and the dream 'I'm going to where it'll be much easier' Roger moved to live in the 'big smoke' where all 'the action' was. For years money jangled in his pockets as he drifted from one job to another. Work was easy to find in a variety of warehouses or factories, labouring outside in all seasons, as well as being employed both in front of and behind the counter at cinemas, cafes and restaurants. He was adaptable and developed many skills in each setting where it was always 'hands on'. However, he never gave any thought to his future.

Roger had met and married Miranda who'd been a barmaid at the local pub. She hated the place and was desperate to leave at the first opportunity, which happened to be when Roger appeared. One baby after another arrived in quick succession. Renting was the only option for him to keep a roof over the heads of his ever-expanding family.

Today was the weekly family outing to the local shops. All four children, aged from two to eight, eagerly anticipated what they were going 'to help' retrieve from the shelves 'to throw' into the trolley.

"Mum, I'm ready. What's on the list?" came the excited voice from the eldest child.

Three more young voices loudly echoed, "Me too." "Me next." "I want to help too."

Roger pushed the trolley and Miranda glanced at a very long shopping list.

"Tommy, one big pack of toilet paper please. Ruby and Jonathon, a big box of tissues each. Barbara, a small packet of cat and dog food please."

Everyone wandered down to and entered Aisle One. But all four children looked up at their parents with eyes and mouths wide open. Something was wrong. There was not one solitary item to be seen; no toilet paper nor any tissues.

"What's going on?" exclaimed Miranda and Roger in unison.

"How much toilet paper do we have at home?" Roger queried with concern.

"Enough for today and tomorrow," stuttered Miranda.

"Ok, so we're alright for a day or two. I'll have a look elsewhere later on today on my way home from work," Roger quietly murmured to his wife.

Not wanting to show any panic, Roger gently guided his children back out of that area. "It's alright, kids, let's go see what is in the next aisle," he said more calmly than he was feeling.

The family moved into the second aisle. There the shelves held all the usual requirements for pets. All four children assisted in that aisle and the next few.

However, when they reached Aisle Ten, once again, the shelves were bare. "Mum, what are we going to eat tomorrow morning? Our breakfast boxes at home are empty?"

"I want my Cornflakes."

"I want my Weet-Bix."

"I want my Porridge."

"I want my Coco Pops." All four children whined, whinged, and whimpered in unison.

Roger knelt down and looked at each child. "It's okay. Dad will find some later today after I've been to work. There are lots of other shops I can go look in."

Continuing on throughout the remainder of the shop, there were many more partially filled shelves too. Quietly both Roger and Miranda wondered why it was like this today. The family was only able to purchase half the items required from the very long shopping list; hence, instead of the normal trolley load, this time it was only partially filled.

As everyone helped to empty the shopping into the boot of the car, Miranda and Roger looked at each other.

"I promise, we'll be alright. Give me the shopping list and I'll go looking after work today," Roger quietly murmured. "I'm grateful I have a job and we have money to go shopping."

Six months earlier, Roger's employment opportunities had dried up for the first time ever. He was directed to talk with a Job Provider, who sent him off to complete a Certificate Three in

Individual Support for Aged Care and Disability. He'd been terrified. As a child he'd detested going to school.

Many thoughts surfaced in Roger's mind, including 'I can't do this,' and 'I'm a fully grown man but now I am being told I have to go back to school.' But times had changed.

As a mature-age student, and on the first day at the course, Roger wanted to bolt out the door and never come back. But deep within his body, he knew his family depended on him. Sitting on one side at the back of the room, Roger looked around at the other students. Everyone ranged in age from their twenties through to their early sixties. One other bloke also sat in the back row but nowhere near Roger. Neither acknowledged each other. So here they were: two blokes in a room full of women, being forced into a course they did not want to participate in.

Ten weeks later as the theory segment ended, both blokes had thawed and became firm friends. The women embraced their presence too. Contact details were shared between all twenty students as they embarked on the compulsory three week Prac. Emails, texts and phone calls zinged, dinged and ringed as they supported each other through the practical component of the course.

On Roger's final day, he was nervous when the Aged Care Facility Manager offered him part-time work, starting immediately on the following Monday morning. Roger surprised himself in his new career as a Care Worker. And both staff and residents were happy to see him appear through the door when he was rostered on.

"Does anyone know why there's no toilet paper or cereal at the shops?" he asked in the staff room.

"Haven't you heard?" someone answered while staring at him in amazement. "Didn't you hear it on the news this morning? There's rumours a new virus has erupted overseas and it's about to arrive like a tsunami here in Australia."

"No. We don't have a TV and we rarely put the radio on. Years ago, I made a decision to tune out of the relentless onslaught of bad and sad news that comes on all forums of media; newspapers, big screens as well as the small ones," he replied. "I'm grateful I am a family man. When I'm home I play with my kids and help my wife. I have no time nor need media of any description in my life."

"Well, people are panicking and many items are being flung into fully laden trolleys. Unfortunately, it looks like those people and their trolleys have been caught up in the undertow of floodwaters; the staff have been unable to stop them from disappearing over the horizon," another staff member added.

That night when the kids were in bed, Miranda and Roger talked about the current crisis that potentially could escalate.

"I have a family who I am proud of and love being with," began Roger. "I have a job with money trickling into the bank each week. With our budgeting skills we always have and will continue to make ends meet. I refuse to get caught up in all the drama and panic that is being unleashed out there in our community."

"But what is going on?" cut in Miranda. "I'm scared."

Roger continued. "Today at work, I was told there's a new virus about to arrive here from overseas. They've nicknamed it 'The Felix Scooby Virus."

Miranda cut him off. "The What?" she exclaimed while staring at him.

Roger replied, "Apparently it originated from countries where they eat cats and dogs. So, it's being called 'The Felix Scooby Virus', as in Felix, the cat, and Scooby Doo, the dog".

"How could they?" wailed Miranda. "Why would anyone want to eat our Lady and Leo?"

Roger took a deep breath. "Miranda, calm down. No one's going to eat our pets. They are safe. But remember, I grew up on a farm where animals were born and sold to be eaten. Look at us, we both eat the meat that comes from cows and sheep. Every country is different. Just remember, not so long ago there were other serious outbreaks. Mad Cows Disease came from consuming infected cattle products. Unwell birds and poultry caused Avian Flu. Sick pigs were responsible for the Swine Flu. Eating the flesh from wild animals was where Ebola came from. It now seems the origin of The Felix Scooby Virus has come from those who were anywhere near or consumed animals, including cats and dogs, that were kept alive in cages prior to slaughter. Miranda, I have often considered not eating meat anymore. However, now I *am* seriously considering becoming a vegetarian.

"I've also discovered The Virus is spreading rapidly and infecting people all over the world. Some are seriously unwell and are taken to ICU in hospital. The numbers of those dying are increasing, but the good news is most people recover. There is a rumour that we are also headed for a Recession or Depression like never seen before in Australia; potentially many people will be out of work soon. And who knows what other doom and gloom will be cast in our direction."

Roger paused to gather his thoughts.

Miranda wondered, wide eyed, what was coming next.

"You and I, we are like glue; joined at the hip. Together we will and can get through this. I have been through many tough times, both before I met you and since we've been together.

"Do you remember when we met, I told you about the farm I grew up on?"

Miranda nodded. "Yes, and you told me all the paddocks were given names. I remember laughing so much because I didn't believe you. Babies and pets are given names but surely not paddocks!"

"Ours did. That was normal. But I understand you found it very strange. Can you remember what I told you about The Green

Paddock?"

With a surprised voice, Miranda replied, "Good heavens, no. Of course not!"

Roger smiled. He quietly and calmly told her he'd be back in a minute or two. Picking up a pile of paper from the desk in his study he slowly wandered back out to Miranda.

"A few years ago, I began putting pen to paper … actually, it was fingers to the keyboard. I have written about my time on the farm. I haven't finished it yet, but here is a small section that I want you to read right now."

Miranda loved reading, so there was a sparkle in her eyes as she focused on the first page.

Journal Entry for Boyhood Memories of a Farm by Roger

Nearly everything on the farm was given a name; pets, working dogs, milking cows, calves and orphaned lambs being hand reared. Even the farm itself had a name; ROBENTON. *My dad used his imagination by combining the names of his three sons; Roger, Ben and Tony.*

It flowed naturally to name every paddock on the farm too. An enormous dam for the sheep to drink from was found in the Dam Paddock! The pigs lived in the Pig Paddock! The 360 Paddock was a monster; being 360 acres in size. The Front Paddock was divided by a long sandy driveway that I walked along from the house to the main road to catch the bus to school. There was also the Lake Paddock, where a natural fresh water lake was filled with living paperbark trees. Residing in both the water and trees were a variety of two and four legged animals of all shapes and sizes. Many feathered creatures from all over the world flew into and out of the lake based on their annual migratory cycles.

There were many other paddocks, but for me the best one of all was the one next to the lake. The Green Paddock was covered in nature and would and could never be developed as it was and always would remain a Nature Reserve. My Dad was given permission to purchase it, but it came with many conditions to protect it from human destruction.

I frequently spent time in this natural sanctuary. It gave me a short reprieve and a unique opportunity to be caught up in the wonder of nature, rather than the dramas and ever present work on the farm or at school.

This was a place devoid of human noise. The Green Paddock offered the luxury of peace and solitude for me as a young farm boy. The frogs' chorus floated through the air from the lake into this paddock. Kangaroos used this area as their bedroom. The dew drops glistened on the many silky spider webs cast between the scrubby foliage but unfortunately sometimes the sticky strands wrapped themselves all over my face or arms if I accidentally blundered into them. When I sat still there were always beetles, flies, moths, bees and butterflies to watch out for, along with swooping birds looking for suitable delicacies to satisfy their hunger. Crickets, grasshoppers and cicadas chirped a merry tune too. And then there were ants scurrying here and there; little ones, big ones and all the rest in between. I enjoyed playing a treasure hunt game to locate stick cocoons hanging from branches in the scrub. How I enjoyed playing the imaginary game of pretending to be an explorer; discovering this wilderness for the first time, over and over again. More to Come Soon ~ Roger:))

Miranda looked up to see a trickle of tears slowly falling down Roger's cheeks, like a snail leaving a silvery trail on a window pane.

Miranda sprung up and wrapped her arms around him. "Oh, my darling, I never realised the farm meant so much to you. And it's still with you, even now all these years later."

She paused for a moment before continuing. "But I do know you are always able to remain calm; nothing ever ruffles your feathers. And then there are times it's like you temporarily disappear; an empty body stands in front of me for a short time, but then just as quickly you re-emerge to being the real you again."

This surprised Roger. "Ahh, so you have noticed. I have been doing that all my life. The Green Paddock gives me a reprieve from the potential stress of the current situation. That patch was a natural sanctuary for flora and fauna, and nature has always had a calming effect on me. This is regardless of whether I am surrounded by nature in person or if I am only recalling the sights, sounds, smells and colours from a long time ago. The Green Paddock has always given me a place to forget reality for a short time before I need to make a decision or solve a problem."

He paused. "Miranda, a crisis is coming our way. It is what it is. Life will go on," Roger continued. "My family is my world, so I have everything that I have ever needed or wanted. We will live from one day to the next, like we always have. There will be many sad, bad and difficult things happen in time to come, but there are always silver linings to look out for as well."

Roger's mind was on a roll. As his mouth caught up with it, he continued.

"Miranda, I've just had an idea. The Green Paddock has helped me enormously during my lifetime. You know how much I love doing things together as a family. I reckon I've discovered a new activity we can all do together. On my next day off, let's go to the National Park up in the hills. There I can introduce and educate you and the kids on how nature is so important to us. We can take the I-Pad with us, so the internet can help us on our Day of Discovery. At long last I can begin to share how I've always been able to Retreat into the Green Paddock."

Maxine Spencer

Those Endless Cups of Tea

My toes twitch as I amble along the hard-packed yellow sand of the placid, inlet waters. After the channel to ocean side of the point, where the wind battered and pummeled me, where salt spray tingled up and down my arms and legs, this side encourages calm, peaceful thoughts and I am returned to a time long ago, to the one day of the year when life was full of family, food and fun – a day to relax after the busyness of Christmas – Boxing Day.

Nine o'clock, on the dot, Tom pulls into the parking place on the hard beach sand. Other cars, laden with families and equipment, follow.

'Come on, kids,' Tom shouts to the gaggle of children exiting from the cars, 'grab everything, otherwise we'll miss our possie.'

He hoists chairs from our car boot, grasps the Esky. I toss the picnic blanket over my arm. Children grab whatever they can, other grown-ups bring picnic baskets, and the men bring the Eskys, some containing food and cool drinks, the important one containing beer.

Soon towels, bathers, hats, beach balls, buckets and spades, Totem tennis, and jumpers, essential for when the wind changes, complete the pile.

Mum and Aunt Mary place cutlery, cups, tea leaves, infuser, and sugar on the card table next to the thermos. Aunty places the infuser into cups, tops each one with near boiling water, adds milk and, together with our cups of tea, we women are ready for the day. Dave, Merv, Tom and Ed open a beer. The younger parents give the usual warnings to the older children, 'Look after the littlies, watch out for cars and stay in the shallows.'

Dad opens the car door for Grandma, puts his hands under her knees and helps to swing her legs out of the car. She hooks her arm into the crook of his elbow, leans on him and shuffles up the slope, balancing on her walking stick, towards her waiting chair.

Seated, she runs her fingers across the armrests, thumb to fifth finger, plays imaginary chords. Practice to keep her fingers supple for her and Joy's piano duets at the Seniors' Concert. Later, when Ed brings out his radio, if she recognises any songs, she will hum the tunes in her contralto voice. We treat her with respect, for her regal manner and appearance demands such attention.

We adults settle down for the day, eager to catch up on family news. 'Did you hear about Will? He is having tests for cancer.'

'He's been sick for a while.'

'Poor Alice. How will she manage with her four and a sick husband?'

We take part in this conversation feeling guilty, some having called him lazy for not wanting to work, but we do not voice those thoughts.

Ed nods his head towards the flick rods lined up like soldiers resting against the tree trunk. 'You going fishing?' he turns to Dave.

'Depends on the wind.' Dave wets a finger and holds it up into the breeze. 'Offshore wind here.'

'Worthwhile having a go, maybe around the point.' Merv peers up the bay to the channel, assessing whether the wind and waves will be up on the ocean side.

Dave and Merv roll their pants up, take a bucket and stroll to the water to go cockling. Because the tide is out; and the beach exposed, they wade well out to ankle deep water, scoop up handfuls of cockles, some for bait, and if you liked them, to take home and boil for a salt and pepper, dipped in vinegar, cockle sandwich.

Later, with their fishing bags containing bait, knives, board, hooks, and sinkers and carrying their rods they will leave us for an hour or two. On an outstanding day they might come back with sand whiting, herring or skippy. We hope they bring back a sizeable catch to be shared amongst everybody.

Tom reads the paper, the horse racing pages. 'Got any tips for this afternoon's races?' He and Ed discuss the odds of various horses, one as an owner, the other having worked with horses in earlier years.

'See what they say about Hi Skies, and Blue Jersey. Both good. I've put a bit on them.'

'What about your horse? Is she running?'

'Yeah, look at race 5. Sound field, but she might get a place.' He hopes she does as he spends copious amounts of money on her.

At the waters' edge the bunch of children swim in the shallows, collect shells, build sandcastles, until coldness, hunger or thirst overcome them.

'I'm starving, Mum,' Yve yells. Other voices follow in unison, 'What's to eat?' the signal to us parents that our broods are about to interrupt our relaxation.

From picnic baskets mouth-watering delights appear, crunchy cheese biscuits, shortbread twirl biscuits, Grandma's Congress Tarts, cordial or cool drink for the kids, and a cup of tea for the adults.

Ed checks his watch, strolls back to his car, stopping along the way to greet a mate and check the fish in his bucket. He nods, satisfied that he can report a reasonable catch to Merv and Dave. He carries his battery-operated radio ready for the start of the races.

A lazy day, an appreciated day, for some of those present work year-round in their businesses. Today, no one talks profit and loss, stock, and staff, tomorrow they will be behind shop counters again.

Lunch time brings a mouth-watering aroma of left-overs from the previous Christmas day: cold chicken, ham off the bone, cut by Dad into sandwich sized pieces, enough for everyone, with sufficient left at home to last the week until another feast on New Year's Day. Aunt Alice opens the bowl containing Ed's fish specialty, fillets of whiting crumbed and fried to golden perfection. We enjoy the coldness of yesterday's baked potatoes, the sweetness of pumpkin, thin slices of bread and butter, cut up tomatoes and cucumber, followed by cold Christmas pudding, all washed down with a cup of tea, and cold cans of beer. Although we have eaten enough, no one can resist the brandy laden slices of Mum's Christmas Cake, baked from an old family recipe.

Dad serves Grandma her meal while she sits in her chair. The sun breaks through the clouds bringing with it the heat. She wipes her handkerchief over her face, pulls her dress up over her knees, and we see her beige almost-to-the-knee pants. As the temperature continues to rise, she hooks her fingers in her garters and rolls her stockings down to her ankles. 'Good looking pins,' we call out, all the while admiring the smooth, English skin of her white legs.

The children organise teams, including a parents' one, for totem tennis. 'Can't we watch instead?' Del screws up her face, pretending dislike for the idea.

'No, Mum, you've all got to play.' Cheers and chortles come from their team at the end of the game when they shout, 'We've won.'

Collecting all the kids, we dawdle to the shop, stopping for a play on the swings, before each child receives a Peter's ice cream bucket, their special treat for the day.

By the time we return, the card table is ready with a pack of cards for those who want to play Poker, or Twenty-one. Mum and

Aunt Mary sip at a fresh cup of tea, Ed tunes his radio to the races, grabs another can and sits to listen to the caller. At the end of the day's races, he will tell us he won, not say how much, but he will go home with a smile on his face. Tom continues to read the paper.

Mid-afternoon, as the sun dips further behind clouds and the wind tugs and tosses our clothes and hair, we pack up. Shaking towels, clothes, and rugs, we grumble about how much sand each child brought from the beach. After a thorough check that nothing remains, we carry our belongings back to the cars.

Those perfect Boxing Days continued through the years, when parents, grandparents, a great grandmother, sisters, brothers-in-law, and cousins gathered to share and appreciate our extensive family structure.

I continue my walk, hesitating to peer at what was once our perfectly grassed possie, now tiered and secured by retaining walls, dotted with benches and seats, where people sit with a take-a-way paper mug of coffee and a bucket of hot chips, and I am wistful for the past, for those lazy, carefree, once-a-year days.

Past the boat-mooring pens, up the bituminised roadway I stroll back to the cabin where my family and I holiday.

The older ones have now gone; we miss the young one who never grew up.

Those other youngsters now address us as Grandma and Grandad, Aunty and Uncle.

Del and Merv, Wendy and Dave will arrive soon; the cups are out each with a teabag, ready to be topped with water and milk. I will hand them their tea, before we sit and talk about old times.

Lorraine Spring

Dark Side of the Moon

Nothing stirs – no leaves tremble in the absent breeze, no bug-eyed creatures hop, slither, or fly between the crater walls. Silence. And Darkness. Not only the absence of light, but black, pitiless nothingness. A coldness that freezes all hope of life, seals the ground from any chance of nurturing one tiny bud of anything. The stale smell of emptiness rolls across the surface, blanketing the tiniest sound. Even the tail of a fragmented comet brings not one speck of light into the treacly morass of darkness. Who knows what microscopic life hides beneath the frozen surface, waiting for the dawning of light? The darkness penetrates the soil, the rocks, and even hope itself. As the moon spins around, only one side, the 'near side' is ever visible from a rotating earth.

Once, a burst of flames shot from Earth to land on the near side. No bird with golden plumage breathed in the oxygen-starved atmosphere of the red planet, and yet the Eagle landed. Out of its bowels came white-suited men who stepped on the virgin surface. Amid the magnificent desolation of its meteor-pocked crust they declared it one small step for man. Heavy boots left footprints that an unchanging atmosphere preserves until mankind makes its next giant leap.

Meanwhile, in the barrenness of space, the earth continues to rotate and the moon to spin, careful to keep its dark side turned away. Man will never know what strangeness creeps across the bleak surface, a strangeness that blossomed from some forgotten microbe that once clung to a weighted boot. That microbe, sterile and lifeless on its home planet, has taken on a new life in the isolated void of the lunar landscape, and now has a purpose. It senses the brightness that awakened it from its dormant state, but it is not enough for it to thrive. And so it starts the long migration to the other side, the dark side of the moon. On its journey it will double in size, then double again until it reaches the shelter of the first crater. Next it will sink beneath the surface of this inhospitable rock and begin the long process of sending out feelers to assimilate the dry ground. Photocells inside its now enormous body change the molecular structure of everything it ingests. Soon it has enough nutrients to reproduce itself—which it continues to do as time rolls by. With nothing to disturb it, this re-generation carries on unheeded.

Beneath the dark surface a heaving, gelatinous mass of life competes for room. Tiny tentacles split from the parent body, and some wriggle their way below ground to the other side of the moon in their search for nutrients. Many struggle to the surface of the planet where their own evolution begins. To extract moisture from the almost airless atmosphere, several creatures develop wings, while others slither along the rocky ground, their bodies developing scales to protect them from the heat. Appendages sprout from other forms, though the bigger they grow the fewer they need. After many failed attempts, one variety stands upright on two of its four appendages. A radioactive shell hardens over the new bipeds, allowing them to thrive in the toxic atmosphere. Their entire body becomes one organ, a unique adaption that allows them to survive and thrive in a place where nothing should.

On the near side of the moon, a fiery blast heralds Phoenix, again not a bird, but a titanium sheeted rocket ship. Man has decided it is time to make that next giant leap and has sent representatives from every nation on Earth. Despite their orders, each man wants to claim the first step for his country. Instead of the one democratically selected, four silver-suited men tumble down the steps to plant their own flag. In the race to reach the one left many years before, no one notices the microscopic tendrils that attach themselves to their lead-lined boots. The stillness of the planet now rings with heavy footsteps. Muffled cries break from the opaque helmets of the competing men. They reach the first flag almost as one person, and jab their own poles beside it, each convinced they have a split second advantage. Hands pump the air in triumph and together they return to the rocket ship. They receive the congratulations of their fellow crew members and share with them the experience of that awe-inspiring walk on the moon. But that is not the only thing they share.

By now the organisms that reached out tiny tendrils to attach themselves to their boots have migrated beneath the skin of each astronaut. In the following days as they return to earth, these organisms will invade the flesh of every crew member. The organisms have learned adaptation is their greatest form of survival and soon will take over the entire body and make it their own. When this happens, nothing will remain of the host creature except his outward appearance. The zombie-like body will continue to function in some limited capacity to enable its alien invaders to reproduce in other life-forms. This transformation will take some time, time enough for each astronaut to return to his own country and, while appearing normal, infect every sentient being on the planet. The giant leap for mankind has begun.

Wendy Stackhouse

We Have a Bridge

We Have a Bridge. Ours, unlike the Oresund Bridge which connects Denmark to Sweden does not unite two countries. That spectacular Scandinavian bridge soars eight kilometres across the Oresund Strait from the Swedish Coast to the artificial island of Peberholm. From there a four kilometre tunnel runs under the sea to the Danish island of Amager. This combined road and rail bridge connects the Danish capital of Copenhagen to Sweden's city of Malmö. The bridge has become an integral part of the transport networks of Central and Western Europe.

Despite finding sixteen unexploded World War Two bombs on the seabed, workers completed the bridge ahead of time. When it opened in June 2000, almost 80,000 people ran across it from Denmark to Sweden to compete in an inaugural half-marathon.

Eleven years later the two countries joined again to produce the TV Series 'The Bridge'. This Nordic Noir series with the flawed detectives typical of these dark thrillers also starred the Oresund Bridge. The haunting music accompanying the opening shots of the sleek bridge spanning the strait, brought the Oresund Bridge into lounge rooms across the world.

We Have a Bridge. It does not share dramatic views across the harbour or Opera House, nor do the locals call it 'The Coathanger' because of its arched design. Sydney Harbour Bridge alone lays claim to these attributes and more.

Our bridge began with less drama than that of the Sydney Harbour Bridge, which, in 1932 had its opening ceremony hijacked by a political stunt. In front of 300,000 onlookers, a member of a paramilitary group rode his horse towards the official ribbon and slashed it with a ceremonial sword. The startled Premier of New South Wales did not even have time to open his silver scissors.

Another rider who claimed his place in history that day was nine-year-old Lennie Gwyther. With the blessing of his father, young Lennie rode alone on his pony, Ginger Mick, 1,400 kilometres from Gippsland, Victoria, to witness the historical event. Later, his hometown Leongatha erected a statue in his honour.

Eighty years ago the bridge's 49 metre clearance allowed most vessels to pass beneath it on their way out from the harbour to the Tasman Sea. With the increasing size of today's cruise ships, this has become more of a challenge. Cruise-ship passengers, drinks in hand, now gather on deck to cheer as the tip of the funnel slips beneath the steel girders with centimetres to spare.

We Have a Bridge. They did not paint ours 'International Orange', like the Golden Gate Bridge of San Francisco. At first the United States Navy wanted it painted in black and yellow stripes to enhance its visibility to shipping in the notorious fogs of the bay. Then the Army Air Corps put in a request for red and white candy cane stripes. The people of the 'City by the Bay' eventually picked its current unique shade, and are happy that their bridge escaped any resemblance to a giant wasp or over-decorated Christmas tree.

The bridge crosses the Pacific Ocean from San Francisco Bay on the south to Marin County in the north. Since its opening in 1937 both people and animals have travelled across the often fog-shrouded suspension bridge. Black-tailed deer once stopped traffic as they wandered through the lanes. Rescued from the slaughterhouse, a six-foot female ostrich en route to her new home kicked her way out of her trailer and bounded between the cars. However, the most frequent animal commuters are coyotes.

They lope over in the dead of night from the north side to the city in search of the odd pet dog or cat to supplement their diet.

We Have a Bridge. So far no one has declared their everlasting love by attaching a padlock etched with their beloved's name onto the handrails of ours. This dubious honour belongs to the Pont des Arts Bridge across the River Seine in Paris.

The original bridge, built in the 19th century at the request of Napoleon Bonaparte, resembled a garden suspended over the river. Flowers decorated the railings, with benches each end for people to enjoy the view. After suffering aerial damage through two wars, they rebuilt it in 1981. The new bridge became a favourite with artists and photographers across the world for its romantic views across the Seine.

For years couples locked padlocks to the railings before tossing the keys into the river as a symbol of eternal devotion. This began to weigh the bridge down and in 2015 authorities removed 45 tons of these metal declarations of love to prevent the bridge from collapsing.

The Mayor of Paris auctioned millions of these unique padlocks for funds to help Parisian Refugees. They built a children's playground with the $400,000 raised by the sale. This gesture must gladden the heart of every Amelie who ever pledged herself to her Louis before throwing the key into the Seine.

We Have a Bridge. Hopefully, ours will never become a 'Dog Suicide Bridge', the nickname for the Overtoun Bridge in Scotland. This stone bridge spans the nearby River Clyde from Overtoun House, a 19th-century baronial mansion in West Dunbartonshire near Glasgow.

Over the past fifty years, 600 dogs jumped the high walls of this bridge to fall 15 metres into the river below. Fifty of these dogs died, but of those that survived, many tried to leap over the ancient stone bricks again and again. For 110 years before this, Overtoun Bridge remained a harmless stone structure. Then in the 1950s, the first dog leapt to his death over the parapet, followed in the same spot by many others.

All the dogs belonged to breeds known for their sense of smell, like Labradors, Collies, and Scottish Terriers. They only jumped on sunny days, which gave animal experts a clue to why these placid pooches ended their lives in such a tragic fashion.

When the experts examined the rough stonework of the 160-year-old bridge they discovered the nests of many rodents, including mink. Introduced from America into Scotland in the 1950s, mink were farmed for their fur. When animal fur fell out of fashion, many of the mink escaped captivity.

Fine weather spread the rank musk odour from the urine of these animals, a lure no self-respecting hunting dog could ignore. Heedless of what lay beyond the high granite walls, one by one these unfortunate hounds bounded the ramparts to seek this compelling scent. Instead, they fell to their deaths on the rocks below.

Overtoun Bridge now has a sign posted each end warning dog-owners to keep a tight hold of their pets. Scotland also introduced a program to cull the mink as an introduced species.

We Have a Bridge. Unlike the Tower Bridge of London, our bridge lacks the bascules, which part to allow ships to pass beneath. Opened in 1894 by the future King Edward V11 and his wife Princess Alexandra, Tower Bridge crosses the River Thames near the Tower of London.

The walkway running far above the bascules became the hangout for thieves and ladies of the night, forcing its closure from 1910 until 1982. Transparent panels installed in the walkway in 2014 now allow foolhardy souls to walk on glass and gaze at the River Thames 42 metres below.

Drama and theatrics have dogged this stately bridge. Several dare-devils flew a variety of planes through the span of the bridge over the years, including an Australian who performed the stunt in his sea-plane in 1919. The pilot of a Royal Air Force Hawker Hunter Jet became the first to fly a jet plane through the gap in 1968 as a protest against the government of the day. Once, a London bus driver hit the accelerator and sped over the one-metre gaping chasm when the bridge parted beneath his number 78 double-decker bus. A similar situation almost caused an international incident when the bridge opened just as President Bill Clinton's car passed. Panicked security guards remained behind while the President's car travelled on unaware. Bridge officials previously tried to contact the American Embassy to warn them of the opening time, but no one answered the phone.

Despite all its dramas, the Tower Bridge continues to be one of the best-known landmarks of the City of London.

We Have a Bridge. The Matagarup Bridge, the first cable sway bridge in Australia, is our bridge. Chosen by the local Whadjuk community, the name Matagarup means a place where the river is only 'leg deep'.

This pedestrian bridge crosses the Swan River from East Perth to the Perth Stadium on the Burswood Peninsula. Sports fans can park their cars, or travel by public transport to East Perth, then walk across the bridge to watch their favourite teams.

The week before the official opening on July 14th, 2018, three hundred of the bridge workers walked, ran, jumped and danced their way along its 400-metre span. This allowed a team from Curtin University to test it through special sensors. Later over 1200 people trotted backward and forwards to test its sway.

The tests proved more successful than those carried out on Central London's Millennium Bridge which closed two days after it opened. The weight of several thousand pedestrians on opening day caused it to swing back and forth like a pendulum.

Having survived every test, Matagarup Bridge allows footy fans to eat their meat pies without a hint of seasickness from a swaying walkway.

At night, colour-changing lights sprinkled throughout the two metal arcs above the bridge transform them into a pair of gigantic swans. With a majestic grace, they shimmer towards each other, mirrored in the river below that bears their name. Perth's beautiful new landmark is a welcome addition to the City of Lights.

And this is our bridge.

Wendy Stackhouse

Runner-up Bronze Quill Award 2018

Seeking My Nirvana

I have always said that if I didn't feel safe in my own country I would not stay here. I have lived in, and visited, many countries and have experienced levels of safety in them. In China, provided I did not fall foul of the Government, I was completely safe. In Bolivia, around 9/11, my motel window was smashed as one person in this small hamlet assumed any female travelling on their own would be American.

The lack of freedom of movement, that I had thought I would always have, along with pandemics, expired Passport and dwindling resources have meant I must rethink just where it is I could actually move to. When I worked in England, Richard Branson's Virgin company had just taken over the railways so I added to his wealth at that time. I doubt he would now consider me a candidate for a free trip into Space in one of his capsules.

Because I did not take the British up on their offer, made twenty or so years ago, to be able to live in their country if I worked four consecutive years with the one employer, they might not welcome me back there.

Even in that quiet very lovely country that is Malta I saw the effects of the beginning of a global crisis, when it was inundated with thousands of people fleeing Libya. Some to stay just long enough until their own country or company got them off this small island refuge. I shared the hotel apartment complex with an Ambassador and his family from an African country. They were waiting there to find out what their Government wanted them to do. I shared the streets with thousands of workers from

Malaysia waiting for their company to move them to the safety of their own country. I saw the ships and the aircraft moving thousands of people to a safe place.

Malta does not have the space or land to grow its own foods so to face the prospect of finding food for thousands, at the drop of a hat, or the brainstorm of some despot, would not make them happy to have a geriatric seeking to live on their small island.

Because of the hard line taken by our Government to deport any people in this country, without citizenship, who break the law, means New Zealand would probably not welcome a geriatric, non-citizen, with open arms.

My short trip to Ireland resulted in my spending days in bed with the gastro they gave me. As well as their stealing one whole hour of my life as Day Light Saving started on my birthday. Those memories are still too new to go back there even to the Family Castle recently restored by money from people in those countries our ancestors had fled to.

The whole world that I had always assumed would be mine for living in has now diminished. The problems of my country with recent weather, fire, drought, flooding and now facing a pandemic and the financial crisis these factors have produced, means I would not probably be welcomed with open arms in too many of our affected towns.

I think I have found the very place, the land that now welcomes older people. It took me a long time to find its location, but two things happened in one day. I watched a TV programme where Judge Judy appeared and was interviewed. Next year her show will have been running for 25 years. She admitted to now wearing a wig to cover her reducing hair line and when I watched her show that very day, I saw an old woman in her TV court room. Judge Judy herself is married to an 85 year old.

That is one place I could live. Where the main actor admits

to wearing a wig. Where all the people in the courtroom, even those appearing with problems, all look lovely and well dressed, and even old women can be sued.

I have been in some of our local courts and few, if any of the accused, come dressed properly. Few courts, if any, have a gallery of well dressed, mostly youngish people with lovely hairdos. Tonight on the news we learnt about toilets being closed for years in the courts' buildings, and legal staff bringing their own soap.

Then there is the possibility of being permanently in the audience of other shows such as Dr. Phil. Not only would I learn how to live my life safely, and healthfully, but being a member of the audience, I would often be given aids to achieve that aim.

This new land, that I have been looking at as a place to live out the rest of my life, is beckoning me. So clean, so safe, so young, so well dressed.

No mention of weather disasters to mar our days.

No problem that does not have an expert in the room, or on the end of a phone, to fix it for you.

Further afield, but not by much, I could line up each and every day as an Extra for any of the films or the TV shows that need crowd scenes; those people that always turn up, who are expected to stay as long as they are needed. Who are fed on the Lot and paid a daily rate whether they are called upon or not. Not much acting to be done by me to fill the role of an old lady pushing her Walker across a street, being knocked down by a car, being robbed of her purse or just lying in a hospital bed, in a scene for the camera, and practising the art of dying.

The card necessary for entry into TV Land and Film Land could be waived whenever they needed a geriatric, true blue Aussie, to fill a part. Like other Australians who go to TV Land and Film Land and forget their way back home, I would be in those safe, clean places, amongst beautiful, young people as I sit in the television audience or perform as an Extra for TV Land or Film World.

Lavinia Tarrant

Where in Heaven's Name Is it?

Ever since people felt secure enough to build chapels, churches, mosques or temples they sited them so that they were central to the daily lives of the believers.

The industrial revolution, that started in Manchester and surrounding areas of England, lead to a plethora of churches in each small town. Local mill owners would provide housing for their workers, a church to worship in and a job for any person professing to be of the same faith as the boss.

In other countries where religions were being introduced to, or imposed upon, the original inhabitants of the area, the churches were built on headlands with sweeping views to see any invasions from the enemy. These buildings provided sanctuary for people in the times of upheaval and danger.

When the world's first cathedral was built, in France, people travelled from all over the world to see this phenomena. It took decades to erect so even the slow travel across the world by ship, or overland by camel or elephant or horse and cart and by shanks' pony, meant people could still arrive in time to see the building being erected.

In many countries still, the church is part of the daily lives of the parishioners. In Chile the churches remain open and people call in for a visit on their way to work, to the shops or to school. The beggars on the steps, with their individual responsibility for selling candles, religious artefacts or maybe going to the family grave of a person who cannot get there and to pray for that person's deceased family members, mean there is security for the church to remain open.

Interest in Churches was overtaken by high rise buildings in the twentieth century and people flocked to New York to see this new phenomenon. They came in ships, by horse and carriage, by shanks' pony and they had the newest inventions of vehicles and trains to get them there.

New countries, such as Australia, adopted the traditions of the country that the majority of the people had left behind. Cathedrals were still central to a city and were sited on high ground and within view of the growing numbers of people migrating to this better life.

In this new country those Cathedrals were erected as soon as the money was raised and the builders, with the skills, appeared. It was important in these new, developing lands, that people knew there was permanency, that sewerage will be laid, that water will be piped, that the huts and tents can be replaced by housing.

Today, in Western Australia in the vast, flat area that is the wheat belt, the tallest thing on the horizon, the edifice that can be seen from distances, is the grain silo. Gone are the days of the long, flat silos where it was possible that only the farm workers, and those associated with shifting the grains, knew exactly where any particular silo might be.

With mechanization, these buildings now rise much higher than any church or cathedral constructed in this country. Just as the churches and Cathedrals were adorned and embellished with icons, these silos are now the backdrop for huge, spectacular painted, art forms.

Today, across Australia, in small towns that have moved on from being settled by generations of the same families, by people involved in one industry, with one or two religions available to the population, few can give you directions to any local church.

I know because I tried, in a small country town, in another State.

Locals were able to point out just where the churches are but have trouble identifying the religion with that building. Staff at centres, once the font of knowledge, such as the Post Office or the local bank, now have people who come from outlying areas to work.

Asking for such directions means you have to take into account the age of the people on the streets or in the businesses. No point in asking the young people, and the younger ones were still in school. Older people, in many instances, are retirees who have migrated to these inland, but close to the great coast, towns.

Men told me with confidence, the name and the location of the pub nearest any church, but not be able to define the denomination of any church within staggering distance.

One older woman directed me to the local RSL Club. "They would know," she confidently predicted. I wondered aloud if Protestants would visit such a place with their pokies? I did try. This was lunch time and the staff were being run off their feet attending to the people in the dining room so I gave up on the idea.

I crossed the road in this small town, which was really not much more than a square of commercial buildings dissected by a railway line to carry sugar cane, and tried the newsagent, but no luck with the young staff – they were not locals. From the back of the building came the answer. Not only the correct church, as in religion, but its name and that of the street it was in.

People flocked to these churches and helped build them, all those years ago when they would have been central to the religious, working and social lives of all the small towns' inhabitants.

No ships were needed to cross the country, no planes available, horse and carts and shanks' ponies would get them there … to the correct church on the right plot of land before the streets were finished.

Those artists decorating the high wheat silos in our State could do the locals a favour by cladding those sad looking churches in their murals: anything to bring them to the attention of the population now working, if not living, near them.

Lavinia Tarrant

Port City

Mid afternoon
a prodigal wind gusts
through heat-locked streets
trailing ten thousand miles
of ocean in its wake.
From tenth floor balcony
city eyrie
I gaze beyond
tawdry two-dollar shops
and fast food outlets
past tracery of cranes
pines like paper cut-outs
to the ocean
a cobalt-blue line
scored childlike
across the horizon.
The tide brims in the harbour
threatening overflow
wind-slapped waves
glass-edged
swollen in full-flood.

Far below
a plastic bag soars
above swings
in the playground
while kids, hair-haloed,
shriek into wind's vastness
as it sweeps across the city.

Madeleine Tingey

Received a Commended in the 2014 Glen Phillips Poetry Prize competition held by Peter Cowan Writers' Centre.

Discovering Maddalena

Journal entries

And so, as the sun dips on the Emerald Coast in Sardinia's north, the music stops by the pool, the singer takes low breaths, the pool chairs are packed, the summer over, the Costa Smeralda is packing up for another year; summer closes its doors and tourist buses turn off their air-conditioning.

But we remember the mountain walks, the cows ringing their bells on the vine-covered slopes, and wonder if the dead of centuries ago could hear the echoes of the funerary, the dolmen stones, carefully placed on the community graves of the Nuragic burial ground. Some 150 people sleep here, the huge crescent-shaped entrance stone, a substitute for a church of the time; its spiritual and meditative powers pre-dating churches. We are awed by the Arzachena Archaeological Park and visit the Nuraghe La Prisgiona with its well and megalithic tower before we move on to la tumba dei giganti, the Tomb of the Giants of Coddu Vecchiu, that Nuragic burial ground, set in peaceful surroundings at the foot of vineyard rows.

We end our journey with a visit to the little seaside village of Baja Sardinia with its memorable cove, where we dip our toes in the sea. Imagine us: walking the beach alongside the beautiful people in their tiny bathing costumes, basking in the sun and enjoying the turquoise sea of an unseasonably long summer. The Costa Smeralda has it all: granites, history and coastline; glorious with its bays and coves and yachts to out-do those of Monaco.

*

On Wednesday 18th September, 2019, we leave mainland Sardinia and take a 20 minute ferry-ride to the famed Archipelago of La Maddalena, with its seven major islands, off the northern coast of Sardinia: bear witness to its spectacular coastal views. The archipelago has been a Parco Nazionale, a National Marine Park, since 1996: the Park is 16 kms in area with a total of 45 kms of stunning coastline. La Maddalena is the only island inhabited since 1770. Water to the island is shipped in. We drive over a causeway, seemingly one lane, that connects La Maddalena - first named after Santa Maria Magdalena in the 16th century then later simply becoming Maddalena - to the uninhabited island of Caprera where Italian hero, General Giuseppe Garibaldi, instrumental in the unification of Italy, lived his last years. Rumour has it that Garibaldi was exiled to Caprera, the island named after the wild goats living there; in fact, he had bought the island he loved and was content to live his last years there.

We enter the house/museum via a small iron gate, step into a courtyard garden and are amazed by the 'easiness' of the house, its beauty, simplicity and warmth, its capacity to hold history in. In the centre of the front courtyard, Garibaldi, a nature lover, planted a pine tree to celebrate the birth of his first daughter, Clelia, with Francesca, his children's nanny. He later married Francesca, his second wife with whom he he'd had three children. His first wife, Anita, Brazilian by birth, had died at the age of 27 in tragic circumstances.

*

The back room of the house contains the elevated bed, where Garibaldi, bedridden toward the end of his life, could see his beloved garden and enjoy views of the sea. Garibaldi died on the 2nd June, 1882: the clocks stopped at 6.21pm; the wall calendar still bears the date; the General at rest. He had lived at the house for 26 years. Clelia continued to live at the house, caring for it and his favourite pieces, after her father's passing. Interestingly, she became a writer, publishing, among other works, her memoir, titled 'My Father' and in 1948 also published a novel, Manilo, written by her father. She died in 1959.

*

In the garden at the back of the house, you will find the Garibaldi family cemetery: Giuseppe Garibaldi's granite tombstone, the graves of his much loved son, Manilo, his little girl, Rosita, who was two when she died. Rosita was named after Garibaldi's beloved mother. His loved Rosa, Anita, Clelia, Teresa and his second wife, Francesca, all buried here.

Rose van Son

Somewhere South

He chops wood, uses the hand saw, eyes off small logs: measures them with his mind; measures the thickness and length, their burning capacity. I collect smaller pieces from the forest floor, stack small boughs; stack them on the verandah for safe-keeping, for the cold.

Sometimes I push a log down with my foot, hold it to the forest floor, one foot tight against litter, fallen leaves mulched from years of discarded branches; cover the damp with pages of past lives. I know insects hide their secrets there.

He saws wood. We saw together. Saw thick branches into manageable pieces for the fire. His jaw firm, his foot hard-pressed on a log, slashes the fallen timber with the saw, draws its fine teeth backwards and forwards. I use both hands, push against the lower level of the branch; follow the saw as it runs on the diagonal, as it rasps in a crevice, tremble as it marks a line there.

Short blocks come off with a kick, sometimes clean, sometimes splintered. He trims what is left. His eyes, quick, then move onto the next piece. He measures it quietly with his mind, measures the length needed to fit the fire, the time it takes to cut the log, the time to burn. Measures how much we'll need to warm a cold winter.

He lifts the logs, holds them gently, like a child, carries them up the verandah steps in the crook of an arm; lays them in neat parallel lines.

We collect wood, wood already measured by the forest as it cleans itself of dead wood, wood discarded by wind in a storm, tossed aside, stories it no longer needs: wood given by trees to make way for new limbs. We rest; sit near the remnants of a burnt trunk. I make notes, write words buried in the undergrowth, watch ants add chapters as fast as they can, watch them lick sap for dessert.

A black stump hides behind the rainwater tank. *This looks good*, I call out. *It will burn for a while*, he shouts. Tension dissolves from his face. He turns the charred remains with his foot; finds charcoal riddled to its core.

Careful there is nothing in it, I say; see a forked tail race along its blackened length. But my voice is swallowed by the wind. He prods the dead stump with his foot, turns it on its head; measures its worth with his mind. Satisfied, the piece passes the test, he picks it up with both hands, strides the short distance to the verandah, adds it to the newly stacked pile. It will be the first to feed the fire.

For another hour I watch him choose and measure, calculate each piece for its value and ability to warm, pieces scattered by wind and fire, pieces left behind after a storm, split and dried, measure its value to insects and mammals, those scratching a living from the damp soil.

The rain draws me in. I pull my jumper close, marvel at the ring of silence, its beauty like pearls, spider webs spun between boughs, lift, layer and stretch between forked branches; imagine the shoots of new spring. I marvel at the season's return and call him for tea.

We leave our shoes outside the cottage door, our home for a time. Sip, dunk biscuits. Gum nuts rattle the tin roof. Tall timbers draw a halo around the house; he stokes the fire, prods it with a twig. Through fogged windows, a rainwater tank reminds us of where we are. We don't know what the weather will do but the wood is cut and stacked and, for now, that is enough.

Rose van Son

A Sense of Place

In the moments before the sun lifts over the horizon, I am on my verandah, looking down on Oyster Harbour. At this breathless time of pre-dawn light, the harbour shows me its shining morning face, a silver plate, still and solid, framed in dark hills.

A questing bird, low to the water, mirrors itself, dark arrow against the sheen. Stick legs scratch the surface, ruffling the molten silver in its passage.

A rippling movement disturbs the ghosts of morning, the prow of a shallop at its head, gliding towards the river mouth. A voice, faint in the never-before-disturbed silence:

"Doucement alors. Prenez garde. Il y a certainement une barre …"

Baudin's marins ship their oars, dripping diamond splinters in the first rays of slanting sunlight.

Baudin leans forward, peering over the side as he searches for the current that will define the river's course.

The rising mist makes wraiths of them all as they drift into the gauzy haze of morning.

Baudin, forever haunting his place in history.

And I, in my place, still watching.

Astra Warren

The Creek

Catholic Mass requires daily attendance and specific congregational response. When the priest chants from the pulpit, those seated reply together. This is listed in the Prayer Book. I do not call this participation. It's an answer learnt by rote. From the unsmiling faces in school uniform no-one shows joy in this house of God. We even mumble the prayers.

The polished Jarrah pews gleam maroon as sunbeams dance on the wood. Sunshine streams through coloured glass windows, depicting more suffering Saints. The church interior is bathed in golden glow, yet it is chilling. I raise reverent eyes to the crucified Christ. His slumped head displays a spikey, thorn crown. His pale chest gleams with crimson blood droplets. Metal bolts through crossed ankles reveal flesh gouged by piercing. How could God be executed? The lingering death of criminals!: Lips cracked panting for air and raging thirst. Why kill a God?

My child face often streamed tears in chapel. Brown eyes spilt water on my white blouse. I glanced furtively at Mary's statue in the corner. She glowed with motherhood and youth. Mother to God and yet her blue cloak was simple. What an amazing career option. Sister Flora hissed at our class.

"Quiet, girls, it's morning prayers. Girls, kneel, clasp hands, just listen!"

Sister was always dour, tired, and impatient. Round of face, bosoms, hips, she moved clumsily. She swayed towards me with a ruler and whacked my knuckles hard. My boney four-year-old knees ached on the cold planks. "Quiet, Kerry! We do not chat in church."

My classmates snickered but quickly hushed as sister hovered near. Now cross, she was red, sweaty, and bushy eyebrows met in a single line above pale eyes. She leaned over and the chunky wooden cross swung before my eyes as she whispered intently, "Jesus is watching you." I opened one eye to see if he was staring at the class.

My German Gran had selected this convent for my Kindergarten learning. My red curls bounced on the collar of my white blouse. No style, I pinched Dad's Brylcream to flatten them before class. Gran brushed them daily to detangle, but my green·bows slid off. I began the day neat and ended it minus socks, leather shoes, and green jacket. Gran despaired when I tossed my case on the kitchen floor then hastily scampered down the backyard to the spreading Mulberry tree. I should obey her.

"Kerry Anne, back here right now and change."

My grandpa had died 5 years earlier. Coalminers never grew old. I believed the black coal dust must have covered his insides so blood stopped moving. He was a jovial Irishman and loved gran's scones. He talked with animation in a rush, arms waving, eyes wide.

We had moved from the city to live with Gran, 'cos now she was old and lonely. But we did not make her smile. Her grey hair, pulled through a foam donut, was pinned in a bun. She wore black or grey all year.

I tried to love her, yet she knew no stories, games or songs – not even *Jesus Loves Me*.

My pop's lounge chair was olive green with wide arms I could sit on and tickle him. I knew he was dead, but did he miss me in heaven? What job could he do there as he liked to be busy?

He had 3 strands of white hair stretched across his head, with tufts over the ears. Stocky body, blue eyes. He leant forward to hear the radio news at night. No one is allowed on his chair. It is empty and alone in the corner. I was three when he died and heaps of townsfolk came to his meeting at the cemetery and threw dirt into the grave hole. Why did they not shovel it? Much quicker and less messy. Red roses on the coffin stayed there. I wished I could visit. Even if we only had Milo together in heaven once.

Gran's home was oiled weatherboard with a silver tin roof. It had very large rooms with high ceilings and flowered plaster ovals around the pendant lights. The grey curtains matched the grey Axminster carpet with pink camellias all over. She had no joy in her comfy home, except to keep it scrubbed and the laundry cement troughs filled with fresh flowers. She was a florist. Gran did funeral wreaths and huge bridal bouquets. A central circular posy, with three trailers of wired flowers, almost to the bride's shoes. Tuber roses, daisies, frangipani, fishbone, and maidenhair ferns were a fragrant rustle on silk skirts. Her orchard had red plums, nectarines, quinces for stewing, black grapes on a trellis, green apples and root vegies. The fuzzy gold peaches were my favourite, but I spiked it on a fork, so the fuzz stayed away from my fingers.

Honeymoons were not allowed for World War II troops. They returned to combat in a few days. If nobody wanted war why did they keep on killing each other?

I was smacked with a wooden spoon at home when naughty, for talking with mouth stuffed. This was the era of rationing. Bridal wear was simple, and practical, to be used later. Veils were replaced with smart hats. Makeup was scarlet lipstick, rouged cheeks, and natural curls. Fresh flowers could be pinned in hair and rings were often family heirlooms of sentimental value.

Mum's gown was white crepe, pin-tucked bodice, slight train, and huge bouquet of white roses and gardenias fringed with fern. She had black hair and dark eyes with the oriental beauty of her mother. Nan Burgess was of Chinese descent, Brisbane market gardeners or fishermen. Small with olive skin, flat features and almond eyes, to me she was just Nan! To state I never noticed she looked different seems odd. To me, she was loving, poor, a servant to her family and devoted to her red-haired Scots husband. Loud, humorous and bawdy he was the exact opposite. In their marriage, they never owned a home, travelled or went out for meals. She budgeted carefully 'cos Pop was an accounts clerk all his life. He was her world … then I and my mum, her only surviving child. The son, Clifford, a bomber pilot, was shot down on his first mission over Germany on a night flight. I have his last letters to Mum. They ached with loneliness, fear, frustration and awareness of impending death. It was a goodbye.

Discipline was strict in my home. Quick slaps for rudeness. No treats for laziness and no chance of shirking family chores. We were a team in which all helped.

The convent used a ruler on hands. We had prayers morning, lunch and home time, and I could recite lots real quick.

I told my mum I was unhappy and so was she. She told dad and next year I was changed to a school with boys, joined classrooms, big oval, basketball courts and toilets where you could pee by yourself. I didn't complain anymore. This government school made me smile; so I did well, in reading especially. Loved art with poster paints and we could have class news once a week – stand by teacher and show a bug in a jar, plant, photos, new shoes etc. My dad said now I was too chatty and made his ears droop.

Amaroo was a bustling Primary School where my aunt was Headmistress. What luck! I only had time out for chatting lots. I preferred this to all subjects – a neat worker, diligent, busy, but so talkative.

On the way biking home, I stopped every second afternoon at a burbling creek. It gurgled through marshy land with dense reeds beside it. Many mosquitoes hovered in the spicy clumps of watercress. Water was icy cold in winter. After tossing socks and school shoes on the bank I waded in. My toes crinkled blue, teeth chattered, yet I sang softly to myself.

In June, with overcast skies, rain showers and singing frogs, this was my favourite place. School day was over. Time to empty head of subjects and join nature as me.

My toes squelched in the mud, feet cooled quickly in the shallow, clear stream.

I used my white, plastic lunchbox to chase tadpoles, splash water, and empty cake crumbs for the ants. They were glad and brought their friends to afternoon tea. This was my special place of fun and pure frolicking. Mum knew of this adventure when I happily rode home with a basket full of dripping cress. I had dribbled green juice when I sucked the porous stem and munched a few leaves like a contented cow. A frog chorus was the only sound. I had a sense of place in unity with nature. Solitary play without talk. I was the eldest of three: two younger brothers argued, teased, and borrowed my treasures without asking. I kept mind images of smashing their trucks, ripping books, or binning Meccano pieces. Conscience prevailed mostly. I was supposed to be responsible, mature, and kind to them.

My ribbons slid off pigtails. Face and hands were grimy with gritty sand. I collected in a plastic bag some smooth, grey pebbles. They might form the base in my aquarium I was planning for the study. A few mottled brown frogs leapt from the rushes to land silently on the bank, prodded when my toes found them in the mud. They were startled, not angry, or fearful. However, their bulging gold eyes seemed worried. Should I abandon cress for a frog collection in the lunchbox? They were lively, mobile and noisy and required little training. They were not huggable, but I knew their appeal as a choir at dusk, although my two brothers were loud and uncooperative. Also we had roaming chooks with one rooster guarding during the day. Did they fancy frogs? I must ask my biology teacher on poultry diet. I was the egg-collecter each arvo, then returned them clucking to the pen. Eggs were layered in my apron pocket. Three or four usually for Dad's breakfast. Other jobs were feeding Binky, the dog, his evening meal. He showed joy with small barks and a dance around his metal bowl before gobbling. I dressed him up in Sally's bonnet, (my best doll) and a white scarf fetchingly looped about his shoulders. Often I would throw his red ball on the front lawn and tackle him to the ground in my best Rugby move of the day. He would not skip in the rope with me, or pick oranges from the orchard, but he was my best pet. The boys wanted to ride him as their Pinto pony in cowboy games. He was a small Kelpie-cross – ginger and black with a tail which circled. He could hide under the house if they became too demanding, or I would lock him in the garage and say he had gone to bed early.

To this day, I have never picked watercress again. It is an era lost.

Kerry Westlake

A Day Never to Forget

After my two-hour bullet train journey south from Kyoto I was ready for my much-anticipated visit to the infamous city of Hiroshima. Exiting the Shinkansen, a waft of humidity greeted me. I wasn't sure what to expect. I located the correct bus that would get me to the Peace Memorial Park. Along the way I saw a city vibrant with life and the scars of yesteryear barely a feature.

As soon as we pulled up just before the bridge even the untrained eye could spot the skeleton, the A-Bomb or Genbaku Dome on the edge of the river. The carcass of the lone surviving structure after the atomic bombing of Hiroshima on the 6th of August 1945. It mesmorised me from the start as I clambered off the air-conditioned bus and back into the heat.

A quiet symbol of the destruction of war surrounded by the normality of every day Japanese life. The exposed curved metal dome skeleton perched on top of what was left of a grey concrete and red brick building. The rest of the crumbling brick work scattered within the interior of the structure seen through vacant windows and doors. The whole ex-building once thriving, has become a symbol of the destructive capabilities of man and for some a symbol of striving for peace. It is surrounded by a black wrought iron fence and in some sections a vibrant green hedge.

The sight helped me to internalise the vast devastation of what had happened here. This scene juxtaposed with the lush green grass and the moss-covered trees was a sign of the regeneration that had occurred since. Next to the A-Bomb Dome was the river, several plaques and statues, and various pathways with the occasional cyclist. Small clusters of tourists wandering around and peering over the fence to take their photos or selfies across and around the fenced site.

As I moved around the fenced area my view of the crumbling structure changed. The rubble within and the various shapes and shades allowed me to appreciate the memorial from each angle seeing more shattered parts of the building and remembering the shattered lives of those who would have been going about their daily lives in Hiroshima at the time the bomb dropped.

In my stroll around the memorial I was stopped by a dear Japanese woman who offered me a paper crane, the symbol of peace she told me.

"We all hope for peace one day," she said, and I couldn't agree with her more.

I tucked away this supremely special gesture carefully in my backpack and continued on around the circular fenced skeletal dome pausing underneath a large tree. That gift from a stranger and an act of unexpected kindness made me smile.

To my right was a circular water fountain with red flowers that I decided to photograph and as I was framing my shot a cyclist rolled into my viewfinder.

I was a little annoyed to tell you the truth because often you have to wait for the photo frame to be free of people and this guy had – ruined my shot!

The cyclist directed his bike close to the tree trunk I was standing beside and I returned most of my attention to the dome. In my peripheral vision I did notice the guy hop off his bike and remove a layer of lycra. It was now increasingly hot and the humidity oppressive and it was still early in the day.

He fiddled around and I gazed at the dome marvelling at the continuing changes that a different angle of view made.

Then he made his approach with a pink slip of card in his hand and asked me if I knew about the history of the atomic bombing of Hiroshima. His English was clear but at times broken, and he was unimposing, though I was still unsure of this complete stranger in a foreign land. I had by this time been in Japan for nearly two weeks but still as a woman travelling alone it was always best to be cautious. Even in broad daylight.

However, I didn't want to be rude, so I admitted that I had just arrived and part of my being here was to learn more.

It was then that he revealed that the pink card was his birth certificate and that he was in fact a survivor of the bombing. He paused for a moment allowing me to react. I was shocked and awed that survivors of the bombing were still alive (history not being my strong suit I wouldn't have known either way).

Then he continued to clarify holding the pink birth card out for me to view, "I was in my mother's stomach…"

Again, I had never really thought about this either and I said as much.

He asked me if I had seen the cemetery and some other sites and I shook my head knowing that I would make my way around the park for the rest of the day.

He nodded and gestured to me to follow him, "Come I will show you."

Then he tucked his birth certificate inside his backpack and proceeded to march off in the direction he'd come. I followed him speechless as he left his bike with his backpack, and his pink slip birth certificate parked up underneath the tree. All were unsecured – no locks or chains, no friends to watch over the precious items. And although I had seen people leaving bikes unlocked in Japan, this was different.

We crossed the road over to what looked to me like houses and came to a stop at a small hip height a pillar that had old roof tiles attached to it.

"See this is rough and that is smooth."

I nodded and ran my fingers over the historic roof tiles;

indeed, some surfaces were bubbled and lumpy and rough whilst others were obviously smooth.

"Radiation," he said.

I marvelled at the evidence of a time that to the uneducated one would not have noticed, certainly I wouldn't have realised the significance strolling through the streets of Hiroshima on my own.

"Have you seen the cemetery?"

I shook my head and immediately he headed off further down the road and into a small cemetery which was located on the same road. In this one small courtyard were about fifty headstones made of various kinds and colours of granite. He pointed to some surfaces facing certain direction, "The radiation made these rough."

He encouraged me to feel the headstones, indeed some surfaces were rough and others polished up granite as originally made and recognisable as a headstone.

I absorbed his words and the understanding of how the radiation bomb had affected this place started to sink in. You knew the radiation direction just from looking at these headstones.

"Have you seen the drop site?"

I shook my head, "No not yet."

In the back of my head was this dear man's bike and backpack still unattended blocks away and most certainly out of our sight. But he clearly was unconcerned and once again said, "Come I will show you."

Then we walked onward around a few more corners to stand in front of an unassuming plaque the site where the bomb was dropped on Hiroshima 6th of August 1945.

It was here I got a photo of my unexpected tour guide.

Then he said, "Come I will show you more."

He took off at a brisk pace and crossed the road and the river and headed to the next must-see spot.

Set off by a wide walkway in one straight view from the war museum on one side to the A-Bomb Dome on the other side was our next port of call. An arched memorial within a rectangular watery body. This arched memorial is what is called a Cenotaph which is an arched tomb for those who died because of the initial blast or exposure to radiation years later. Below the arch is a stone chest holding a register of these names, of which there are over 220,000. Some floral tributes on either end of the water feature had previously been left to honour the lives lost on that dreadful day in history.

It was at this point in my impromptu one-on-one tour that I noticed the tour groups. One after the other coming in hearing the spiel of their tour guide about this special place and then after a few moments moving onto the next must-see sight.

I was truly grateful to be able to walk around the park with my new friend and tour guide. He was able to answer my questions and tell me stories about the real people that these events in history had affected. I was able to learn and to absorb the history in the way that no documentary or book could ever do.

Close to the rectangular war museum my new friend pointed out two trees also bearing the scars of the bomb. He explained that half of the trunk of the tree had been exposed to the radiation and disintegrated, leaving a hollow centre. Despite this the tree continued growing and flourishing incorporating the scars of the past into its being.

After that we walked some more, across some internal roads within the peace park amongst the shade of the trees. Despite the numerous trees there was not a leaf out of place here and I realised why as one older gentleman collected rogue leaves and raked the ground beneath the lush green canopy.

We came to another memorial this one smaller, more intimate.

"This is for the Koreans who died in the bombing."

A black stone memorial pillar with an engraved message sat on top of a tan stone tortoise. The tortoise was draped with folded paper cranes and surrounded by circular stonework and floral tributes.

We walked a short distance and came to a sunken area in the ground which was surrounded by stones of various sizes. In the centre was a square pillar of stone and beside it two stone spheres which I gathered weren't originally like that. My Japanese friend explained that the sunken ground was the original level of the ground prior to the bombing, now two feet below the current ground level. He also explained the stone pillar and how the round stones topping the rectangular base had fallen off due to the shock wave. Because of his explanation I was able to notice the detail in the scene and appreciate that the ground we had been walking on was made up of the radiation debris the bombing produced.

Next, we visited the Children's Peace monument with the display of many thousands of folded paper cranes. Years after the bombing one little girl Sadako Sasaki while sick in hospital due to the radiation poisoning started a revolution. She set herself the goal of folding a thousand origami paper cranes and now children from all over Japan take up the challenge and also together fold a thousand paper cranes. A reminder and a symbol of peace in Japan.

Next to this is a memorial arch of Sadako and her folded paper crane surrounded by two other children and a bell that can be rung beneath the arch.

My gift of the paper crane earlier in the day now made more impactful with the understanding of this story. The reason, the why behind the delicately folded piece of paper.

Finally, after hours dashing between significant sites and many a story my tour guide took me into the air-conditioned foyer of the war museum and introduced me to another invitro survivor of the bombing. It was here our impromptu tour of Hiroshima's Peace Memorial Park came to an end.

My dear host bid me farewell and returned to his bike. And I was left stunned at the amazing experience I had stumbled upon. My capacity to understand each exhibition in the museum was heightened by my personal tour around Hiroshima.

But Hiroshima was more than just a bucket list item or something to check off my holiday to do list. On my trip to Hiroshima I learnt so much about people, which is exactly what I had hoped for.

Specifically, I witnessed a better way of treating people through this man's generosity with his time and his stories which were a gift to a complete stranger. These memories will stay with me forever, along with the haunting tales of the bombing.

Mankind can on the one hand be so destructive and cruel and on the other we can be brave, courageous, and kind. I sure know which way of life I want to live. This is what Hiroshima and all its residents are now ambassadors for – the way of peace.

Cheryl Workman-Davies

Antarctica

An infinity of white
Comprised of vast beauty undulating yet still
Dramatic craggy ridges and crests
Ice covered mountain ranges
Juxtaposed against
Iridescent blues of the depths below
By land awkward waddling penguins
By sea powered through the water by jet propulsion
A place of danger and creeping glaciers
Breathtaking vistas and water bound creatures
This is the seventh continent
Antarctica

Cheryl Workman-Davies

Japan

Neon lights
A rainbow of colours

Bursts of lucky red
Accents of glinting gold

Vibrant, loud, hordes of people
Ordered, functional, dynamic

Culture, tradition, fashion, future
Writing in pictures, Karaoke for songs

Old mixed with new woven together
Temples and shrines sprinkled all over

Polite and humble, plus a bathing ritual (Onsen)
Graceful and peaceful, known for Sakura (Cherry Blossom)

Natural beauty all around
The occasional rumble from below the ground

Bamboo, rice, peaches and plums
The bounty of the fields the countryside yields

Cheryl Workman-Davies

About The Society of Women Writers WA

The Society of Women Writers was first established in Australia in Sydney in September 1925, to bring together women writers and journalists in New South Wales. Their aims were to be a social body; to promote knowledge of literature; to encourage women writers; and to strengthen the ties of interest between Australian and visiting writers (www.womenwritersnsw.org/history/).

Until the 1970s, the Society was based in Sydney, using a postal critiquing system to keep in touch. During this decade, branches were established in other Australian states and the first Federal Constitution was adopted in 1978 with an agreement that Federal responsibility be transferred from state to state every two years. Twenty years later, the decision was made to decentralise, with each state forming its own Society.

The WA branch initially operated only through correspondence groups until the first President, Ethel Webb, was appointed in 1981 and members began to meet regularly. The Society of Women Writers WA was incorporated as an autonomous body on 25 February 2000.

Contact Details

The Society of Women Writers WA Inc
PO Box 434
Northbridge
Western Australia 6865
Tel: 0415 840 031
Email: swwofwa@gmail.com
Web: www.swwofwa.com.au

www.ingramcontent.com/pod-product-compliance
Lightning Source LLC
Chambersburg PA
CBHW070605170726
48291CB00003B/713
* 9 7 8 1 9 2 2 3 4 3 4 5 1 *